Early Independ
Of The
Maidenhead Area

Written and published
by Paul Lacey

An unusual and impressive coach was this 1949 Foden PVSC6 with Wadham bodywork for the Alpha Coaches fleet of W.F. Carter & Sons of King Street in Maidenhead, seen here at Wembley Arena in red, blue and cream livery.

Written, designed, typeset and published by Paul Lacey

17 Sparrow Close, Woosehill,

Wokingham, Berkshire, RG41 3HT

ISBN 978-0-9567832-6-4

Printed by Biddles Books, King's Lynn, Norfolk, PE32 1SF

CONTENTS

ACKNOWLEDGEMENTS

A work of this nature, researched on-and-off over 50 years alongside other projects, has involved input from many sources, so my apologies are tendered should any go without acknowledgement here. Generally, I have spent much time perusing the local newspapers of the time, so thanks to the Library Staff in Maidenhead and Reading, along with the Berkshire Archives. I am also grateful to my fellow researchers for making available information they had gleaned, as well as my contacts at the Omnibus Society and PSV Circle. Much personal information was also taken from the Census, work I undertook often parallel to my own Family History activities.

However, such a history would be largely unrecorded had it not been for the personal contributions of those who were there at the time, and indeed those active in such operations. In that respect, much very interesting material was provided during interviews with members, relatives and employees of the Bunce, Carter, Clinch, Fuller, Harris, Quelch, Smallbone, Warwick, Winkleman and West families.

I am also appreciative of the photographers, both past and present, who have kindly made available their prints to use in this book, along with assistance with appeals from the Maidenhead Advertiser and use of its Archive.

THE EARLY INDEPENDENTS SERIES

This volume is the final one in a trio covering the independent bus and coach operators in various parts of the Thames Valley area, with the first taking in the Henley and Marlow Area and the second the Bracknell, Crowthorne & Wokingham Area. All are based on many years of detailed research, much of it making use of personal interviews with many primary sources now lost to the passage of time, along with a unique collection of local photographs, preserved here for posterity. These works will complement the volumes already published on the independents of West Berkshire (as the *Newbury & District Motor Services Story*) and the pre-1939 Reading Area coach operators (within *Smith's Coaches of Reading 1922-1979*), along with the volume on the *White Bus Services* of Winkfield. Generally, they cover the period from the pioneering days through to the Second World War, though each operator is dealt with according to its own date parameters and the available information. The activities of the *Thames Valley Traction Co. Ltd.*, and its forebear the *British Automobile Traction Co. Ltd.* already has its own series of volumes.

INTRODUCTION TO THE MAIDENHEAD AREA

The Thames-side town of Maidenhead is 28 miles west of London, 12 miles east of Reading and 9 miles south of Henley, an important river crossing on the Bath Road (A4), so with transport links back to the mail-coach era, its stone bridge opened in 1777. A place long associated with the pleasures of boating and its famous single-arch brick-built bridge on Brunel's Great Western Railway, it had all the enterprises of a small town, with a 1921 population of 16,741, but no specific industries. Much of the surrounding area was given over to agricultural or large country estates. However, between the two world wars a number of areas grew under development, resulting in a large increase in population, a process continuing after WW2, much of that shaping bus operations.

To the north, the Cookham rural area was in fact a collection of small settlements, along what were often quite restricted and unmade roads, which also saw development inter-war, so leading to specific links by local men. To the south the villages of Bray, Fifield and Holyport also contributed operators serving their local communities and adding further colour to the transport scene.

Although the buses of the *Thames Valley Traction Co. Ltd.* provided most of the trunk services, many smaller communities first gained a bus link through the many independents. There were also longer distance links through Dorney and Eton Wick to Eton and Windsor, whilst the *Great Western Railway Road Motors* had several spells of activity centred on the town. With the development of the Slough Trading Estate other routes sprang up to take workers from both Maidenhead and the villages traversed en route.

On the coaching front, the *British Automobile Traction Co. Ltd.* made its presence known early on, and once *Thames Valley* was formed, the Maidenhead Garage had an allocation of coaches until the early 1960's. However, there soon appeared a number of local men, who often undertook such work in addition to other trades, some haulage, taxi or as coal merchants, so by the mid 1920's the town was well provided for. During the next decade many faded for one reason or another, with just a handful left by the outbreak of World War Two. More retirements and takeovers led to the situation whereby *Carter's* would prevail as the sole survivor beyond the 1960's of that once vibrant scene.

Paul Lacey, Wokingham

January 2021

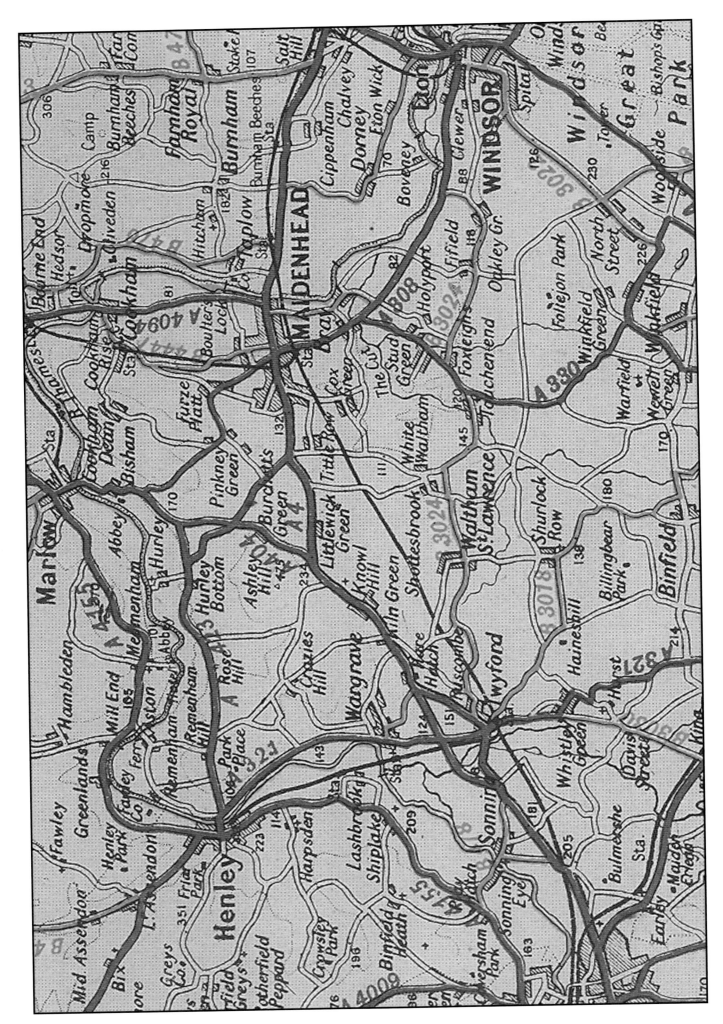

Edward Archibald Burr
Mrs. Gertrude S.J. Burr
Lion Motor Coaches
Maidenhead, Berkshire

Edward Archibald ('Ted') Burr was involved with transport in the Thames valley in four distinct phases over the years.

Born in Bow, East London in 1886, he first comes to our attention in 1911, when he could be found living at 'Lillville' in Reading Road, Pangbourne, Berkshire, from where he provided a carrier's service of some 5.5 miles into Reading towards the east. It started out from Ye Olde George Inn and was run on a daily basis, and his terminus in Reading was at the White Hart at the junction of Oxford Road and St. Mary's Butts, from where he returned at 4.30pm. No details are known of what he used on this service, though a motor vehicle seems likely in view of other known factors, and at that time he was living with his widowed mother.

Soon after the outbreak of the Great War he enlisted in the Army at Reading on 30th November 1914, and he was naturally posted to the Army Service Corps in the 273rd Company Mechanical Transport, being sent to France in September 1915 attached to the 21st Divisional Supply Column as a lorry driver, described in his summary record as a 'good motorman' when de-mobbed in May 1919.

It should of course be noted that within the 273rd MT Company were none other than *Alf Smith* (who would form *Smith's Coaches* of Reading), *Tom Herring* (of *Herring's Coaches* of Wokingham), and *Bill White* (*White's Coaches* of Reading).

After returning from the war he married Gertrude S.J. Cope at Hungerford in West Berkshire in the Spring of 1921, and they had daughter Joyce and son Jimmie in 1924 and 1927. In March 1921 he joined the *Thames Valley Traction Co. Ltd.* as a bus driver from its Maidenhead garage, then residing very close by at No.10 Bridge Street. The latter was a temporary lodging used for new employees without somewhere to live, but by May 1922 he and his wife had relocated to No.5 The Broadway (see map page 92).

However, in June 1926 he left the *'Valley'* in response to the opportunity to drive an ex-WD Daimler Y-type charabanc (BH 9268) for the Marlow-based *Rupert Batting*, which ran as *The Kingfisher*. As it was also used at other times as a lorry on household removals and furniture deliveries, he undertook all those duties.

At the end of 1928 *Batting* decided to give up the chara work, so *Ted Burr* then put all his various experiences to good use and set up in his own right as *Lion Motor Coaches*, based at his Maidenhead home still at No.5

The Broadway, his first advertisement appearing in the Maidenhead Advertiser of May 1929.

Unfortunately, only limited details are known of his fleet, though a Thornycroft (quoted as UU 9685), new in 1929 is accredited to him. However, that registration was actually carried by a Dennis G-type not owned by him. That was followed by a Bedford WLG-type with 20-seater coach body (GP 62), which had been supplied in July 1931 by *Clapham, Roberts & Wallis* of Gerrards Cross in Buckinghamshire, and which was sold by him in October 1941. What seems to have been his final purchase was a 20-seat Duple-bodied Bedford WLB (JB 5937), new to him in March 1935. Painted dark blue, it was kept at the Marlow Road Garage, as indeed the earlier ones may have also been stabled.

Ted Burr was recalled by old Maidonians as a kind-hearted, generous and courteous man, who was also a keen supporter of the British Legion

Throughout the 1930's *Lion Motor Coaches* continued to feature amongst the declining number of coach operators based in Maidenhead and, after *Ted Burr* died at the age of 51 in January 1938, his widow *Gertrude* ran the firm through to about 1947, after which the local directory entries ended. Indeed, the 1935 Bedford is found elsewhere in early 1949, though *Mrs. Burr* did not pass away until 1969 at the age of 84.

At his funeral there were representations from his old comrades of the 273rd, *John Chastell* (*Dean Coaches,* Cookham Dean), *Alf Smith* (*Smith's Coaches,* Reading), *Fred Crook* (*F.H. Crook,* Booker), *Tom Herring* (*Herring's Coaches,* Wokingham), plus floral tributes from *Try & Harrison* (*Windsorian Coaches,* Windsor), *W.F. Carter & Sons* (*Alpha Coaches,* Maidenhead) and *A.D. Hooper & Son* (*Three Lilies,* Maidenhead), as well as the local Taxi Owner's Association and even his old customers from his Marlow days.

The Local Kelly's Directory advert for Lion Motor Coaches for the 1932 edition, which was repeated without alteration through to 1940.

W. F. Carter & Sons
The Alpha, Alpha Coaches, Carter's Coaches
Maidenhead, Berkshire

The well-known firm of *W.F. Carter & Sons* and their *Alpha Coaches* of Maidenhead were a familiar part of the local scene for over 60 years, but both that fleetname and, indeed, the overall business had their origins with others.

On the business front, *William Frederick Carter* had inherited an already well-established enterprise as a Jobmaster, through his marriage to Phoebe Eliza Meeks in 1894. Her father James based his operations at The Greyhound pub at No.47 in the High Street, going back to at least 1871, hiring out horse-drawn vehicles of all descriptions, including flys working the taxi rank at Maidenhead Station. Business was good, with many businessmen who travelled into London or Reading, but were resident in the better areas of the town being regular customers.

As to James, he had not been born locally, having come from Westerham in Kent, being a widower twice before the age of 50, first marrying Elizabeth Favell in 1864, then her sister Eliza in 1871, actually not so rare a situation in a time of higher mortality. He had come to Maidenhead by 1871 as landlord of The Greyhound and later set about setting up the business of Jobmaster in its yard, the first reference to him as a carriage and fly proprietor being in 1883. Various types of vehicles were added, so he could furnish them for beanfeasts, wedding or funeral parties, and of course the motive power of the horses could easily be switched from one type or another without the whole vehicle being off the road. James was joined by his son Arthur (born 1873) to become Meeks & Son, and at 1901 Arthur and his wife were residing at No.93 King Street, whilst the 1903 local directory shows both addresses in use.

In the meantime, *William Carter* had been born in 1869 at Wilton in Wiltshire, moving around with his family, the census returns revealing their progress between 1872 and 1882 through Oxfordshire at Ipsden, Dorchester, Chalgrove and Watlington. But by 1891 his father had taken a position as a butler at Bray in Berkshire. At that point 22-year old William became a representative for the Nicholson's Brewery of Maidenhead, and in those pre-motorised days his job involved riding a horse out to pubs to elicit orders. One of his points of call was The Greyhound, which was run by James's daughter Phoebe, so that is how they became acquainted. After marrying they set up at No.7 Wellington Road in Maidenhead, with William's brother Richard (born 1878), a clerk at the brewery as lodger.

Typifying the mode of transport used for outings in the days before motorised vehicles was this large brake, seen taking employees of Sutchbery's Stores out to Burnham Beeches for their annual picnic.

James Meeks passed away in 1907 at the age of 64, and the 1911 directory shows that by then *William Carter* had replaced him as the entry for flys etc., the business address being No.93 King Street. That had of course been the address for son Arthur Meeks, but at the time of his father's death, the rest of the family had emigrated to Australia, so he decided to continue in the trade, but only as an owner-driver. The son of William and Phoebe Carter, of the same name was also not involved in the business, being in 1911 a 16-year old clerk in a timber yard near the station. However, the reference 'Late James Meeks' appeared in all adverts for some years after the transfer. The Carters then had 5 daughters, plus son Reginald James (born 1910), and both boys would join their father in due course.

The business of fly proprietor continued, with the cab rank by the Clock Tower on Station Approach being the main focus of activity, but by 1917 the stables and yard of The Nag's Head nearby in Grenfell Road was also in use.

With the start of the Great War, there was a sudden loss of many of the horses, whilst young William had been in the Berkshire Yeomanry, so he went off to serve in the Machine Gun Corps for the duration.

With that conflict over, advertising from 1919 noted carriages of all descriptions were available, including brakes for beanfeasts, but now added were open and closed motor cars, including those specifically for the funeral business which would operate for many years. Horses were also kept for use by the Great Western Railway Parcels Delivery Service, which Carter was an agent for, as well as for the local Fire Engine!

Very few details are known of the cars used by Carters over the decades, but this fine line up on Station Approach may contain some owned by them. Left to right they are a Fiat or a Scat (BD 1106), a Lorraine Dietrich (LH 3660) and a Unic 12/16hp (BL 2705), the latter new in September 1912 and painted green.

TELEPHONE No. 293.

W. F. CARTER

(Late JAMES MEEKS,)

JOB MASTER & FLY PROPRIETOR

OPPOSITE CLOCK TOWER,

KING STREET, MAIDENHEAD,

And Nag's Head Livery Stables,

Grenfell Road.

———

HORSES & CARRIAGES

OF ALL DESCRIPTIONS

To Let on Hire.

ORDERS RECEIVED FOR G.W.R. 'BUS.

———

FUNERALS   FURNISHED

WITH GLASS OR OPEN CARS.

———

Brakes for Beanfeast Parties. &c.

CLOSED AND OPEN MOTOR-CARS
FOR HIRE.

The advertising by Carter remained static for years, this 1917 example unaltered after the War had ended.

The first motor known as owned was in January 1916, a Ford Model T with dark blue-painted landaulette body (BL 4732), still in use at 1921. Indeed, William senior got his first driver's license in November 1913. Son William married Bessie Warren in 1919, and by 1927 they were living at No.93 King Street. However, by 1921 land in Bell Street was in use as the base for the motors, with approval from the Borough Council for the storage of 60 gallons of petrol, increased to 250 from October 1922, showing how the motors had now taken over, and the business was poised for further expansion.

In the meantime, various people in the town had started to operate motor charabancs, which at least initially the *Carters* had not been involved in. One of those was *Stanley Collins* of No.7 Marlow Road, who had added to his original *Alpha* charabanc of May 1921, a second 14-seater from July 1922 as LW 4396. He also added a 'speedy 1-ton van' over the Winter of 1922-3. Full details of these activities will be found under his own heading, but he decided not to continue with that trade for the 1923 season, so from the Spring of 1923 the *Alpha* charabancs became the property of *Carter*.

It is worth noting that most charas of the period tended to carry their fleetname across the rear panel, as on the nearside there were many body details, such as doors, to make signwriting difficult, though under *Collins* they had *The Alpha* in plain lettering on the sides. But under *Carter* ownership several are shown in photos with '*The Alpha No.1 or No.2*' emblazoned on their sides, though not in the order they had been procured. *Carters* had added a 14-seater chara on GMC chassis by May 1923, so that might have also been the speedy 1-ton van referred to by *Collins*. A third Crossley was added during 1923 as NO 6432, another ex-WD 25hp WO-type, which came via an Essex operator, and had a 14-seater chara body by Munnion of Chelmsford constructed in July 1922, though later re-bodied

Under *Carter* the range of excursions for 1923 was much the same as the pattern set by *Stanley Collins*, and it is a possibility that he came to work for them, but unfortunately his whereabouts by then are not known. The local tours, coastal excursions and outings to the ever-popular horse-racing meetings kept the little fleet busy, along with private hire, whilst a motor hearse was available from December for that final excursion.

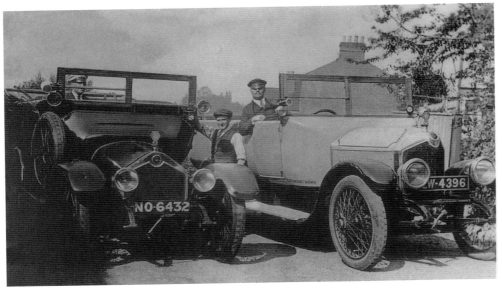

Posed for the camera are two of the Crossleys, which show the differences of the WO-type 25hp as NO 6432 and the 30hp X-type as LW 4396, the latter known as the vee-radiator type for obvious reasons. It is also evident that Collins had not used a standard livery, nor are any details available for the earlier fleet under the new ownership. The driver on the right also appears in Thames Valley photos with its charas.

One of the funeral cars was of the Crossley X-type, but all that is known is that it was not one of those also used as a charabanc, though the registration is indistinct in the photo. Similarly, the GMC removals van offered for hire from the same time is most likely to have been the one also used for charabanc work, but its identity is not known. Also, worth noting is that the capacity of the charas was often ignored, especially when the load consisted of people of varied ages, so a children's trip on a 14-seater might well produce around 20 in all, mostly little ones with a couple of mothers or helpers. In the early days it was also not unusual for there to be a seat on the right-hand side of the driver, as the chara bodies were wider than the original lorry-type chassis, though in due course that was sensibly outlawed!

Another photo seemingly taken on the same occasion, has Crossley WO-type BL 8538, now lettered as 'The Alpha No.2', with Driver Joe Beckett at the wheel.

1924 was, of course, quite a boom year for all chara operators within striking distance of the very popular British Empire Exhibition at Wembley, and *Carters* were offering 3 trips a week from April onwards, that on a Wednesday leaving later, and returning later too, for the benefit of shop-workers on early-closing day. All excursions now left from The Bell Hotel opposite the Railway Station, and those touring the local area continued well into Autumn, if the weather obliged.

Enquiries were also solicited from bowling, cricket and football clubs, and the many social groups which were to be found listed in local directories, many taking their outings with social clubs, fraternities or church connections, often for their first taste of the sea-side. It is evident that expansion was quite rapid between 1924 and 1926, at which point 6 advertised excursions were offered on a single peak-season day. A Dennis 20-seat of around 1925 was evident, but its full identity has not been discovered. There was also a larger Dennis of 28 seats, probably on an ex-WD chassis, also only known from photographs. However, probably by the 1925 season a Reo 'Speed Wagon' had been acquired from a Surrey operator (PC 9504), new in May 1923 and with a 14-seater charabanc body of unknown make.

An advantage of the lighter types was that they were fitted with pneumatic tyres before such equipment was developed for heavier types, and indeed the Crossleys had from new Rudge-Whitworth wheels with wire spokes, just like cycles, so they could easily be changed. Several photos confirm that it was the practice to carry several spare wheels to facilitate a speedy changeover if a puncture should occur, then the driver need only get out the repair kit or find a garage during the layover period, if on longer journeys.

Although the firm was now firmly engaged in the motor age, it nonetheless kept a traditional going through to at least 1928, each Ascot Race Week running a Four-in-hand coach to the course, as was done from several other local areas, as there remained some nostalgia for that mode of travel in that connection. Also, with the racing theme, motor charas were run to all events at Hawthorn Hill, a few miles south of Maidenhead for the Pony Racing, something which continued through to the 1960's in fact.

The legend *Alpha Motor Coaches* in use by the 1926 season, whilst Butcher Mr. Keen at Furze Platt had been added as a Booking Agent north of Maidenhead.

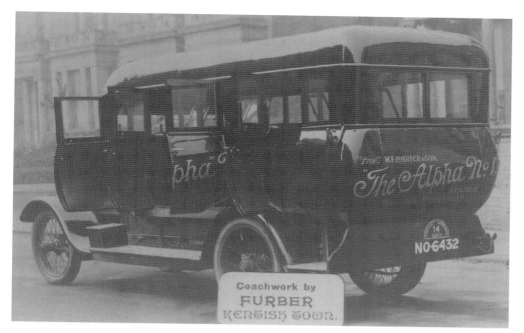

The seasonal nature of the use of open charabancs was obviously a limiting factor, but there was also potential for work over the Winter months in transport sports team, whist parties, darts teams and for theatre visits, so Carters had a new body built at the Furber coach works in Kentish Town on Crossley NO 6432 in late 1923. This enclosed body also featured electric lights, with blankets to keep the chill out, so a useful coach in that new guise.

Further expansion presented itself for the 1928 season, when another local small operator decided to give up on that seasonal trade. The activities of *Edwin Hodsdon* are more fully chronicled under his name, but he had tried such work during 1927 with a 20-seater Dennis 30cwt on pneumatic tyres registered as PP 7694 in March 1927, known as *The Wooburn Belle*, after his base at The Bell pub on Wooburn Green. *Carters* were evidently most pleased to add this fine coach to their fleet, running it in that guise for several years, mainly for its goodwill value, before a repaint and re-naming as *The Maidenhead Belle* for the 1930 season.

By 1927 the excursion adverts for *Alpha Coaches* in the Maidenhead Advertiser occupied more column inches than any other operator, though the town still had a number of smaller outfits, some originating well before *Carters* took to such work.

One of the Crossleys inherited from *Collins* was BL 8538, which continued in ownership of *Carters* through to September 1932, when it was scrapped. However, it cannot have remained in its original format as an open charabanc beyond the end of 1931, so it may have been rebodied, or used in another capacity?

The subject of a livery has already been touched upon, as not even the two vehicles from *Collins* carried the same scheme. It is believed that the maroon inherited with BL 8538 continued to be used for the mid to late1920's, but the first new vehicle for which such detail can be confirmed is in 1931. RX 8407 was new in March as a Petty 20-seater coach body on a Commer 'Invader' 6TK chassis, and it was in a white and black livery. The subsequent secondhand purchase of a 1930 Guy OND with Hoyal 20-seater body (RX 6850) in late 1937 notes it as repainted to cream and black, but the Commer had received a new scheme of two-tone blue by its withdrawal in June 1945.

By 1931 *William Frederick Carter* was living at No.13 Park Street in Maidenhead, whilst the growing fleet was kept at the Old Bell Brewery Yard in Bell Street. During 1930 the business address had been renumbered as No.119 King Street. William's son of the same name (born 1894) joined him in the business by 1927, then as *W.F. Carter & Son*, but by 1931 it was *& Sons* with Reg (born 1910) now also involved, though William senior passed away in June 1932.

With the passing of the Road Traffic Act 1930, a group of excursions and tours was licensed to start from The Bell Hotel, with coastal full-day trips to Bognor Regis, Bournemouth, Brighton, Eastbourne, Littlehampton, Hastings, Southampton and Worthing, day trips for horse-racing at Ascot, Epsom, Hurst Park, Goodwood Races, Kempton and Sandown, plus to Oxford, London, Aldershot Military Tattoo, Virginia Water, Hindhead and Finchampstead, with a maximum of 5 coaches in use on any one day.

The Reo 'Speed Wagon' PC 9504 at The North Star pub with a mixed crowd on a private hire.

In another view of Crossley BL 8538, we can clearly see the scripted signwriting used when with Carters.

The 1930's seem to largely be a period of steady development, but of particular significance was the licensing of a seasonal Sunday express service between Maidenhead and Portsmouth from June 1932, the departure being at 8.15am, with a return at 6pm. Not just popular for day trippers to Portsmouth and Southsea, but also for the ferries to the Isle of Wight, useful for longer holidays with period return fares, and Mr. Emony of Castle Hill was now a booking agent.

It is unclear if any vehicles for the early 1930's have gone unrecorded, but an interesting purchase in 1934 saw a Leyland 'Lion' PLSC1-type enter the fleet, new in May 1927 to *County Motor Services* of Stakeford, which had passed to *Scottish Motor Traction*, then to AEC Ltd., in a dealer capacity. Its original body was by 1934 past its best, so it was married up with a 28-seater rear-entrance body built by *London General* on an R-class AEC 'Reliance', those vehicles then being rebodied from coaches to service buses by Weymann.

TY 3085 is shown at the races as Alpha Coaches with the LGOC coach body now fitted, and it stayed until the end of the 1936 season.

A new purchase for March 1937 was a Bedford WTB-type, which carried a Willmott 26-seater coach body with front entrance, registered as AMO 320, which was to remain in use until November 1948. It made a good impression, leading to other similar purchases.

At the end of 1937 the opportunity arose to buy a 20-seater locally, one that had not seen much mileage in its 7 years' service as a staff bus at Jealotts Hill with Imperial Chemical Industries. RX 6850 was in fact one of a pair of Guy OND-type saloons with bodies built by Hoyal of Weybridge, though *Carters* only retained it for less than a year.

Up until the Second World War the advert in the local directory used the same printers block as widely found of a normal-control coach. Post-war, it was replaced by this half-cab variety, though whether representing an unknown member of the fleet or not is not known.

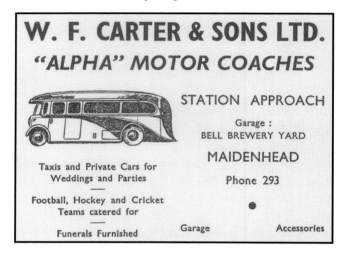

After the Construction & Use Regulations came in with the 1930 Act, the older types of coaches had to be replaced, but the exact fleet make-up throughout the 1930's is not fully recorded, as it was also a period when much secondhand stock was in good supply.

The next recorded purchase came during the War years, when a Bedford WTL-type with Duple 26-seat coach body (JB 5209) of 1935 came from *E.J. Sargeant* of Slough *(Slough Coaching Service)* in February 1942. It will also be found with its original owner *Albert Warwick* under his own heading. During 1943 a WTB-type with similar body new in 1937 came from the London SW19 operator *Adnams* as DUU 714. During September 1945 the firm was granted a utility-bodied Bedford OWB-type in recognition of its contract work, registered as CRX 648. All this trio would enjoy long working lives with the firm, staying until 1950, 1955 and 1958 respectively, whilst the Commer 'Invader' with Petty body bought new back in 1931 (RX 8407) remained through to June 1945, latterly transporting Prisoners of War on farm work from local camps.

There was indeed much war-related contract work in the area, with army camps, airfields and a number of shadow factories, including aircraft production nearby at Warren Row, plus many smaller workshops taken over for war production. At other times, vehicles were called away for transport of troops, sometimes gone for days on end, and invariably at very short notice.

Extract from the obituary of William Frederick Carter Maidenhead Advertiser 22nd June 1932.

We regret to record the death, which occurred in the early hours of Friday morning (17th June), of Mr. William Frederick Carter of King Street, the well-known jobmaster, taxi and charabanc owner, who had carried on business for many years near the Station Yard at Maidenhead, being known to practically every person in the district. He passed away peacefully in his 64th year, after several years of suffering and weakness through diabetes, which he bore very patiently.

The late Mr. W.F. Carter senior belonged to the County of Wiltshire, but came to Maidenhead many years ago, first as an outside representative of the brewery firm of Nicholson & Son Ltd. About 30 years age he started (sic) business for himself in King Street as a taxi and coach caterer, and as a furnisher of funerals. Since those early days the business has grown extensively, and Mr. Carter, always a keen man of business, had improved upon his opportunities and kept pace with the increasing demands of the travelling public for taxi-cab services and the later developments of charabancs, which ousted the old horsed coaches.

Such a business, open nearly all hours, occupied Mr. Carter's whole attention, hence he had no time for identifying himself with any 'public' work, but all the same a busy traffic-business man, he became widely known, and his name was a household word in the town. That he was regarded as a good employer was testified by the genuine regrets of all his connections and workmen, drivers etc., when the sad, but not unexpected news, went round that the disease had finally conquered him.

He leaves a widow, 3 sons and 7 daughters, and we understand that the whole of the aspects of the business will in future be carried on with the same prompt attention by the 2 elder sons, Mr. William Frederick junior and Reginald James Carter.

Amongst the long list of mourners attending the burial were many from the local business community, also from The Oddfellows, along with the Cab Inspector of the Great Western Railway based at Maidenhead.

Transcript of the original application under the Road Traffic Act 1930 for Road Service Licenses as submitted in April 1931.

J.478 Application has been made by Messrs. W.F. Carter & Sons, Maidenhead, for a road service license to run a group of excursions and tours, at inclusive return fares only, starting from Bell Hotel, Maidenhead as follows:-

(1) Day excursion to **Brighton,** via Bagshot, Guildford, A321 to Horsham, Henfield and Brighton, returning same route.

(2) Day excursion to **Southsea**, via Bagshot, Farnham, Petersfield and Southsea. Returning same route.

(3) Day excursion to **Worthing**, via Bagshot, Guildford, Horsham and Worthing. Return same route.

(4) Day excursion to **Littlehampton,** via Bagshot, Guildford, Milford, Petworth, Arundel and Littlehampton. Returning same route.

(5) Day excursion to **Bognor,** via Bagshot, Guildford, Milford, Petworth and Bognor. Returning same route.

(6) Day excursion to **Goodwood Races**, via Bagshot, Farnham, Liss, Rogate, Midhurst and Chistleton. Return same route.

(7) Day excursion to **Southampton,** via Reading, Basingstoke, Winchester and Southampton. Returning same route.

(8) Day excursion to **Bournemouth**, via Reading, Basingstoke, Winchester, Lyndhurst, Boscombe and Bournemouth. Returning same route.

(9) Day excursion to **Eastbourne,** via Bagshot, Guildford, Horsham, Cowfold, Lewes and Eastbourne. Returning same route

(10) Day excursion to **Hastings**, via Bagshot, Guildford, Horsham, Cowfold, Lewes and Hastings. Returning same route.

(11) Day excursion to **Oxford**, via Henley, Nettlebed, Shillingford and Oxford. Returning same route.

(12) Day excursion to **Epsom Races**, via Staines, Laleham, Walton-on-Thames, Esher, Leatherhead and Epsom. Returning same route.

(13) Evening tour to **Aldershot**, via Bracknell, Bagshot, Frimley and Aldershot. Returning same route.

(14) Half-day tour to **Ascot**, via Touchen End, Winkfield and Ascot. Returning same route.

(15) Afternoon and/or evening tour to **Virginia Water**, via Touchen End, Ascot and Virginia Water. Return via Egham and Windsor.

(16) Afternoon and/or evening tour to **Finchampstead**, via Touchen End, Bracknell and Crowthorne. Returning same route.

(17) Half-day tour to **Sandown Park Races**, via Windsor, Staines, Walton-on-Thames and Esher. Returning same route.

(18) Half-day tour to **Kempton Park Races**, via Windsor, Staines and Sunbury. Returning same route.

(19) Half-day tour to **Hurst Park Races**, via Windsor, Staines and Walton-on-Thames. Returning same route.

(20) Half-day and/or day trip to **London,** via Taplow, Slough, Cranford, Chiswick and Marble Arch. Returning same route.

(21) Half-day tour to **Hindhead,** via Touchen End, Bracknell, Bagshot and Farnham. Return same route.

(22) Other excursions and tours on **special occasions**.

Trips Nos.1 to 5 and 7 to 11, 15, 16 and 21 April to October. Trip No.6 July. Trip No.13 June. Trip No.12 April and June. Trip Nos. 17 to 20 all year round. The maximum number of vehicles to be used on this group of excursions and tours on any one day is five.

> *The regular adverts placed in the Maidenhead Advertiser chart the progress of the firm and its range of excursions, but sadly due to poor-quality microfilm copying, few are clear enough to reproduce direct from the source material. Indeed, the situation has more recently been made even worse, as 'new technology' means it is now relatively quick to find references, but the copies are of very low resolution! For those reasons, the following are included as transcripts of adverts from the first decade of coach operation.*

May 1924   The Alpha Motor Coach Tours

Wednesday June 4th, to **The Derby**. Leave Bell Hotel 10am. Return fare 10/-.

Thursday & Friday June 5th and 6th, to **Epsom Races**. Leave Bell Hotel 11am. Return fare 8/6.

Whit-Sunday June 8th to **Southsea.** Leave Bell Hotel 8.30am. Return fare 10/6.

To **Ascot Races**, June 17th, 18th, 19th and 20th.

And to **Aldershot Searchlight Tattoo** on June 18th, 19th, 20th and 21st - BOOK EARLY to avoid disappointment

PARTIES going for their 'Summer Outing' should book their dates early and 'Travel in Comfort' by the **ALPHA MOTOR COACHES**. No party too large.

Cricket Clubs, Bowling Clubs, Beanfeasts and other Parties catered for at very moderate charges. Let us quote you now.

In the event of mechanical breakdown, passengers are guaranteed return journey same day.

Proprietor: W.F. CARTER, 93 King Street.

17th July 1926   The 'ALPHA' Motor Coaches

TRAVEL IN COMFORT   Phone 293

To **Kew Gardens** on Wednesday July 14th. Leave Bell 2.30pm. Return fare 4/6.

To **Sandown Park Races** on Friday and Saturday July 16th and 17th. Leave Bell 12.30pm. Return fare 7/-.

To **Bognor** on Friday July 16th (4 seats only). Leave Bell 8am. Return fare 10/6.

To **Royal Military Tournament** at Olympia on Friday July 16th. Leave Bell 3.30pm. Return fare 4/6.

To **Southsea** on Sunday July 18th. Leave Bell 8am. Return fare 10/6.

To **Bournemouth** on Sunday July 18th. Leave Bell 7.15am. Return fare 13/-.

To **Brighton** on Monday July 19th. Leave Bell 8am. Return fare 10/6.

To **Goodwood Races** on Tuesday to Friday July 27th to 30th. Leave Bell 9am. Return fare 10/-.

To **Littlehampton, Southsea and Brighton** on Sunday 1st August, Leave Bell 8am. Return fare 10/6.

Book up now for your Summer trips.

Pay What You Like   Go Where You Like

Booking Office 93 King Street, seats may also be booked with Mr. Keen. Butcher, Furze Platt.

All passengers are fully insured.

Proprietor:- W. F. CARTER & SON

27th April 1927   The Alpha Motor Coaches

To-day (Wednesday) to **Elm Park** (Reading versus Portsmouth North End). Leave Bell 5pm, fare 2/-.

To-day (Wednesday) to **The Zoo**. Leave Bell at 10.30am. Return fare 5/-.

To **Hindhead** on Thursday April 28th. Leave Bell 2.30pm. Return fare 6/-.

To **Aylesbury** (Maidenhead v. Aylesbury) on Thursday April 28th. Leave Bell 4.40pm. Fare 4/-.

An Afternoon Trip to **Stoke Poges**, Chalfont and Gerrards Cross, returning via Beaconsfield on Thursday 28th April. Leave Bell 2.30pm. Fare 3/-.

To **Hurst Park Races** on Saturday April 30th. Leave Bell 12.15pm. Return fare 7/-.

To **Eastbourne** on Sunday May 1st. Leave Bell 8am. Return fare 12/6.

To **Bognor** on Sunday May 1st. Leave Bell 8am. Return fare 10/-.

To **Hindhead** on Sunday May 1st. Leave Bell 2.30pm. Return fare 6/-.

An **Evening Trip** to Burnham Beeches, Beaconsfield on Sunday May 1st, return via Littleworth Common. Leave Bell 6.15pm. Return fare 2/-.

To **Zoological Gardens** on Monday May 2nd and Wednesday May 4th. Leave Bell 10.30am. Return fare 5/-.

To **Southsea** on Thursday May 5th. Leave Bell 8am. Return fare 10/-.

Single fares may be booked to and from any seaside places advertised.

Book up now for your Summer Trips. Pay what you like. Go where you like. Booking Office 93 King Street. Seats may be booked at Mr. Keen's, Butcher, Furze Platt.

All passengers fully insured. Parties catered for at SPECIAL PRICES.

W. F. CARTER & SON, 93 King Street.

July 1928 THE ALPHA MOTOR COACHES

Modern up-to-date 20-seater charabanc for hire – known as the 'Wooburn Belle'.

To **Hindhead** on Thursday 26th. Leave Bell 3pm. Return fare 6/-.

An **Afternoon Trip** on Thursday and Sunday July 26th and 29th, to Henley, Ewelme, Wallingford, Streatley and Reading. Leave Bell 3pm. Return fare 4/6.

An **Evening Trip** on Thursday and Sunday July 26th and 29th, High Wycombe, Princes Risborough, Chinnor, Stokenchurch and Marlow. Leave Bell 6.30pm. Return fare 4/6.

To **Southsea** on Thursday and Friday July 26th and 27th. Leave Bell 8am. Return fare 7/6.

To **Bognor** on Friday July 27th. Leave Bell 8am. Return fare 7/6.

An **Afternoon Trip** on Friday July 27th, Windsor Park, Virginia Water, with one hour and return. Leave Bell 2pm. Return fare 2/6.

An **Evening Trip** on Friday July 27th, Wargrave, Henley and return via Marlow. Leave Bell 6.30pm. Return fare 2/6.

To **Brighton and Southend** on Sunday July 29th. Leave Bell 8am. Return fare 8/6.

To **Bournemouth** on Sunday July 29th. Leave Bell 7.30am. Return fare 11/6.

To **Windsor Park, Virginia Water**, wait one hour and return. Leave Bell 3pm and 6.30pm. Fare 2/6.

To **Hurst Park Races** on Friday and Saturday July 28th and 29th. Leave Bell 12.30pm, return fare 7/-.

To **Brighton, to Southsea, and Worthing** on Monday July 30th. Leave Bell 8am, return fare 7/6.

To **Bognor** on Tuesday July 31st. Leave Bell 8am. Return fare 8/6.

To **Southsea and Brighton** on Wednesday August 1st. Leave Bell 8am. Return fare 8/6.

To **Goodwood Races** on July 31st and 1st, 2nd and 3rd August. Leave Bell 9am. Return fare 8/6.

Booking Office –

93 King Street. Seats may also be booked at Mr. Keen's, Butcher, Furze Platt.

All passengers are fully insured.

Travel in Comfort   **Phone 293**

25th June 1930   **The Alpha Motor Coaches**

Travel in Comfort   **Phone 293**

Modern up-to-date 20-seater charabanc for hire – known as the 'Maidenhead Belle'.

To-day Wednesday June 25th to **Hindhead**. Leave Bell 3pm. Return fare 5/-.

An **Afternoon Tour** on Friday June 27th to Marlow, Henley and return via Wargrave. Leave Bell 3.15pm. Return Fare 2/6.

To **Sandown Park Races** on Friday and Saturday June 27th and 28th. Leave Bell 12.15pm. Return fare 7/-.

To **Hendon (Royal Air Pageant)** on Saturday June 28th. Leave Bell 10.30am. Return fare 5/-.

To **Brighton and Worthing** on Sunday June 29th and July 6th. Leave Bell 8am. Return fare 7/6 or Single Fare 6/-.

To **Bournemouth** (via Southampton) on Sunday June 29th. Leave Bell 7.30am. Return fare 10/6, single fare 7/6, Southampton return fare 7/6.

To **Bognor** on Sunday 29th and Tuesday July 1st. Leave Bell 8am. Return fare 7/6, single fare 6/-.

An **Afternoon Trip** on Sunday June 29th to Newlands Corner and Silent Pool. Leave Bell 3pm. Return fare 5/-.

An **Evening Trip** Sunday June 29th to Bracknell, Finchampstead Ridges, return via Wokingham. Leave Bell 6.30pm. return fare 3/6.

To **Southsea** on Sunday to Wednesday June 29th to July 2nd. Leave Bell 8am. Return fare 7/6, single fare 6/-.

To **Southend** on Saturday and Sunday June 28th and 29th. Leave Bell 8am. Return fare 7/6.

To **The Zoo** on Monday June 30th. Leave Bell 10.30am. Return fare 3/6.

To **Oxford** on Wednesday July 2nd. Leave Bell 2.30pm. Return fare 5/-.

To **Eastbourne** (a few seats left) on Sunday August 31st and September 7th. Leave Bell 7.30am. return fare 10/6, single fare 7/6.

Taxis will be supplied free, on application to convey intending passengers, within reasonable distance of Bell Hotel.

Kindly note change of number, now 119 King Street (opposite Clock Tower Maidenhead Station).

29th June 1932   The ALPHA COACHES

EXPRESS SERVICE
Maidenhead to Southsea
Every Sunday June to September
All coaches leave Bell Hotel, King Street 8am
Depart Clarence Pier, Southsea 6pm.
Single Fare 6/-   Day Return Fare 7/6
Period Return Fare 12/-

To **Southsea** on Thursday, Monday, Wednesday June 30th, July 4th and 6th. Leave Bell 8am. Return fare 7/6.

To **Brighton and Worthing** on Sunday and Wednesday July 3rd and 6th. Leave Bell 8am. Return fare 7/6.

An **Evening Trip** on Sunday and Thursday July 3rd and 7th, to Marlow, High Wycombe, Stokenchurch, return via Lane End. Leave Bell 6.15pm. Return fare 3/-.

To **Bognor and Littlehampton** on Tuesday and Thursday July 5th and 7th. Leave Bell 8am. Return fare 7/6.

To **Hayling Island** on Sunday July 3rd. Leave Bell 8am. Return fare 7/6.

To **Bournemouth** on Tuesday July 5th. Leave Bell 7.30am. Return fare 10/6.

To **Goodwood Races** on Tuesday to Friday July 26th to 29th. Leave Bell 8.30am. Return fare 7/6.

An **Afternoon Trip** to Virginia Water (via Ascot) on Thursday to Wednesday June 30th to July 6th. Leave Bell 2.30pm. Return fare 2/6.

Booking Offices-
119 King Street (opposite Maidenhead Station) Phone 293
Mr. Emony, Newsagent, Castle Hill, M'head Phone 1382
Mr. A.H. Keen, Butcher, Furze Platt, M'head Phone 793

Proprietors:- W. F. CARTER & SONS
119 KING STREET, MAIDENHEAD

The style of advert used for many years from the 1930's through to much later, with only the coach updated in the process. It is, however, a standard printer's block, not based on an actual coach from the Alpha fleet, the same one being used for Lion Coaches in the town.

As far as is known, the firm lost no coaches to the Requisitioning Officers on their tour during 1940, but nonetheless there was a need to re-establish the coach fleet after the War, with new vehicles unlikely for a year or two if lucky.

That situation led to two interesting purchases in the first half of 1946, both Leyland types, but each quite different from the other. By February a 26-seater on a 'Cub' SKPO3-type chassis had been found as RV 7101, new in July 1935 to Southsea operator *Burnett*, duly passing in that town to *Byng's Coaches*. It had a Duple body and stayed until May 1950.

The 'Cub' RV 7101 when new at Duple Motor Bodies.

The other was in some ways more conventional, being a 'Tiger' TS4-type, but with a twist. Its Harrington body featured a full-length luggage-carrier, to house musical instruments when new in July 1932 as UF 8841 with *Southdown MS* of Brighton. It was earmarked to transport the Band of the Royal Marines based at Eastney Barracks, though when not so engaged it did see service on coastal express services. Whether *Carters* ever made use of the extra space for taking any musicians is not recorded, but it remained in use from June 1946 to November 1949.

The 'Tiger' UF 8841 as new, with full-length 'band-box', had the classic Southdown style of that period.

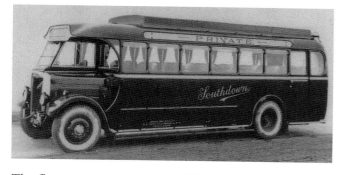

The first new post-war coach followed on with the tried and trusted Bedford series, with OB-type DJB 410, carrying a Duple 'Vista' 29-seater body, which took to the road in September 1946, and would continue with the firm until March 1960.

Several oddities followed, though both are believed to have come from the *Grenfell Coaches*, whose activities ceased at the close of 1946, not a take-over as such, but yet another competitor now out of the frame.

Despite newer types arriving, this pre-war Bedford continued to appear in adverts through to 1952. The livery adopted by 1945 comprised a darker blue with relief in a lighter shade, whilst an Old English style of lettering was used for the fleetname.

One of the coaches obtained in December 1946 had several owners, originating with *Tom Tappin* based at Wallingford, coming over to Maidenhead it is believed for a contract operated by the *Grenfell Coaches*, of which more can be found under the heading of *George Collins*. However, Thornycroft A2-type RX 3633 was new in 1929, so only stayed until November 1947, as it was replaced by another secondhand Bedford WTB. The other vehicle which has little recorded of its movements, had originated with the Halifax-based *Hebble Motor Services* in 1932. CP 9831 was an Albion PW65-type with Brush body, again believed to have passed through the *Grenfell* fleet, which had seen others of that make previously, but it was only kept by *Carters* until November 1947 on a contract job.

Shown below is one of the same batch of Hebble MS PW65's with 32-seater Brush bodywork new in 1932.

With new vehicles still at a premium, more purchases followed of sound secondhand coaches, mostly of the Bedford types already represented in the fleet, with in October 1947 another WTB-type, but with an unusual history. EJJ 269 had actually been built as a showroom for National Cash Registers, fitted out with examples of its products and just a couple of rows of seats, in an otherwise standard Duple coach body! It passed to *Alf Smith* at Reading, and in due course it was fitted out fully for coaching work. New in 1937, it would serve *Carters* until early 1953, with 26 seats in its passenger-carrying guise.

That was followed by another WTB-type, though of the later 1939 variety known as the MkII, again with a 26-seater Duple coach body as FLL 58. It had been new to *Beach's Coaches* of Staines who, like *Smith's Luxury Coaches* of Reading, often hired to or from *Carters* in busy times. It arrived in February 1948 and stayed until November 1955. 1948 saw another trio of WTB-type Bedfords, all with Duple coach bodies and having come through service with *Smith's* of Reading and arriving during November as BDL 111 of 1937, EPP 510 of 1938 and FPU 702 of late 1937, the latter having been built with a rear entrance but converted whilst at the Reading operator to front door layout.

Bedford WTB coach FPU 702 was actually on hire to Smith's of Reading when caught by the camera of Alan Cross at Bournemouth's Avenue Road Coach Park in 1950, alongside a former SMT Leyland 'Cheetah'.

But, despite that, it was not all wall-to-wall Bedfords, as some contracts called for larger capacities, so an interesting couple of coaches were also added during 1948. One was acquired when only 7 months old during September, being a Maudslay 'Marathon' MKIII with Burlingham 33-seater front-entrance coach body as HOM 903, new to Birmingham coach operator *Sandwell*. Despite its short stay with them, it would serve *Carters* until May 1959, recalled as a reliable vehicle with comfortable coachwork.

The other arrival during November 1948 was another interesting coach, actually re-constructed by the North London dealer Arlington Motors, based on a pre-war Leyland 'Tiger' TS7 or TS8-type chassis, which had been re-bodied by Wadham of Waterlooville and given the new registration MMY 164 in December 1946, also coming from *Beach* of Staines. It is shown opposite at the seaside, and remained in the fleet until December 1957.

The Maudslay Marathon MkIII HOM 903 was also in the blue livery, though the relief shade had a bit of grey to it. Note also the side panel with Alpha set in a spray device, also standard throughout the early post-war years. This photo was taken in the yard at the Bell Street Garage, which was in the course of being extended, the outline roof-framing just visible, whilst a Bedford WTB sits in the shade on the left.

The post-war years saw a number of vehicles that had been requisitioned during the war years returning by way of the Ministry of Supply Sales, whilst others such as the 'Tiger' MMY 164 might end up with a dealer to be repaired, rebuilt or rebodied, all adding to the issue of re-equipping war-torn fleets. In that way, *Carters* found themselves getting back to a liking for Dennis chassis, as they obtained a July 1939 'Lancet' MkII with Willowbrook 39-seater body through a Ministry of Supply disposal sale, which had originally been BNR 526 with *Nibloe & Sturgess* of Kibworth, which became *Carters* ERX 432 in March 1949 after being refurbished by the operator and re-registered to them. A photo of this coach appears opposite.

It is not possible to discern from the photograph which model of 'Tiger' MMY 164 had been before being rebuilt by Arlington Motors, most parts being common between that generation of chassis. Arlington replaced the chassis number with an ARL-prefix in order to gain a registration as a 'new' vehicle, not all licensing authorities being so compliant for such issuing of new identities, partly due to tax rules at the time in place to control scarce raw materials.

The refurbished 'Lancet' MKII appears to be having a few problems, if the exhaust emanating from under the cab is anything to go by! On that occasion it was one of 6 coaches on the Southampton and Bournemouth run of the popular coastal express services, and it stayed in service until October 1955.

The next arrival was quite a rarity indeed, presumably offered as a ready-to-deliver vehicle by a dealer? The Sandbach firm of Foden was well-known for its lorries, but it did also market some PSVs at times, though not sold in great numbers, and often associated with the phenomenon of the half-decker coach, which enjoyed a short-lived popularity in the early 1950's. So, it was certainly different for the local area, a PSVC6-type with 33-seater coach body by Wadham, delivered in September 1949 as FJB 406, which ran through to January 1962.

The Foden had a very distinctive front profile supplied by the chassis-maker, and also its Wadham body was a bit dated by then. But, nonetheless, it was a reliable coach, caught at Brighton Coach Park by Bill Haynes.

A pair of new Dennis 'Lancet' MkIII coaches with 35-seater bodies by Yeates of Loughborough followed in February and March 1950 as FMO 482/3, remaining in use until 1961 and 1963 respectively, in fact the last of the half-cab coaches to be operated and, like others still in use, by then in the new livery of light cream, red wings and flash, plus some deep blue, according to body style, but FMO 483 is seen opposite when new.

Another new purchase was a Duple 'Vista'-bodied 29-seater Bedford OB-type as FRX 533 in June 1950, which would remain in use until October 1964, whilst in August 1950 another used WTB-type with Duple 25-seater coachwork arrived as EUW 51, once again via *Beach's Coaches* of Staines.

A further secondhand Dennis 'Lancet' MkII was added in February 1951, being CYC 421 with Dennis 32-seater centre-entrance coach body new in May 1937 to *Ateyo* of Weston-super-Mare, joined that same month by another locally-sourced Bedford WTB DPP 712, carrying a Willmott 26-seater rear-entrance coach body new in June 1937 to *E.J. Sargeant* of Slough (*Slough Coaching Service*), both only staying until 1952.

However, that also brings us to the issue of fleet numbers, which were evidently applied for a period in the early post-war period. Although details are incomplete, notes made at the time confirm allocations as follows, though the list omits FMO 482, despite the inclusion of FMO 483. There is also a duplication listed, whereby EUW 51, which was acquired in August 1950, appears to have taken the number 11 after RV 7101, and 13 presumably was not used. The known list is as follows, including those not confirmed-

Fleet No.	Reg. No.	Fleet No.	Reg. No.
1	MMY 164	11	RV 7101
2	HOM 903	12	?FPU 702
3	DJB 410	13	Not used
4	ERX 432	14	BDL 111
5	CYC 421	15	CRX 648
6	EJJ 269	16	UF 8841
7	EPP 510	17	FRX 533
8	FLL 58	18	FJB 406
9	DUU 714	19	FMO 483
10	DPP 712	20?	FMO 482

We will now take the opportunity to catch up with illustrating the various vehicles joining the fleet during 1949 to 1951, as well as showing some in their subsequent livery of light cream, red and blue.

Rear-entrance bodies on Bedford WTB chassis were quite a rarity, but this Willmott body had been built for E.J. Sargeant of Slough in 1937. It came to Carter for contract duties in the main, but was caught by the camera of Alan Lambert at Bognor Regis on one of the coastal express runs, which travelled via Littlehampton as well, a very popular spot for families in those days.

Centre entrances were also fairly common on Dennis-bodied pre-war 'Lancet' coaches, as here on CYC 421 when new to Ateyo of Weston-super-Mare. Dennis actually built many of its own bodies during the '30's.

Representing the next generation of the 'Lancet' this 1950 MkIII example was photographed at Brighton by Bill Haynes wearing the original livery of twin blues. FMO 483 had a Yeates body and would be the final half-cab coach to be operated by Carters, departing in December 1963 for further service.

The pair of 'Lancet' MkIII's were duly repainted in the new livery of a light cream base, red wings and some blue trim, the latter in the case of these bodies applied as the forward portion of the side flash, noticeable as the darker area on in a photo taken at Wembley – a daily destination for the fleet for many years. Also taken at Wembley is Bedford OB FRX 533 below with 29-seater Duple 'Vista' body, which has the waistrail flash in blue. The new livery wore better than the blue scheme, and as far as the author can recall was unique to Alpha Coaches, but exactly when the changeover took place is not recorded. There were a few variations to its application, and in fact this OB was later given a makeover, which will be seen in due course.

Now we have reviewed the early post-war fleet replacements, we can take a look at what the coaches were employed on. As already noted, the vehicles had been kept busy on war-related work over those years, and it was to some of the same sites that new contracts now opened up. The White Waltham Airfield did still have aeroplanes using it, though it never developed into a more significant airport, as at one time was mooted. However, it was the former RAF hangers and other buildings which now had other occupants, some aero-related engineering, plus others, some of which soon had daily contracts with *Carters* and other operators, The Maidenhead area had also served as a base away from the London Blitz for some organisations, so that would also continue. Other contracts would serve the established industrial estate at Slough, along with new developments to the south-west of the town.

Another factor was the emergence of the Aerodrome at Northolt, which in due course would become London Heathrow Airport. In that respect, the *Alpha Coaches* were a daily sight, as from January 1951 a staff contract ran from the Maidenhead area for BOAC and BEA personnel, funded in full by their Joint Staff Committee, which was still in operation a decade later.

Also requested in January 1951 were additional tours on the existing license to take in the impending Festival of Britain, which opened on 3rd May 1951 (also my birthday), along with football excursions to Maidstone, Epsom, Grays, Tilbury, Eastbourne and Worthing. To further strengthen patronage on the coastal services, additional pick-up points were requested at Braywick (Sawford's Garage), Holyport (Post Office), Touchen End (Hinds Head), Hawthorn Hill and Jealotts Hill (New Leathern Bottel) in respect of Brighton, Bognor Regis and Littlehampton, there being no other operator with those locations. By then there was already a link to the express service from Marlow (Quoiting Square) to Maidenhead for pre-booked passengers.

At January 1951 an existing worker's contract from Slough (Crown Hotel) to ML Aviation at the White Waltham Airfield was renewed, and that was likely to have originated under wartime conditions, at which time the normal licensing procedures were suspended.

For June 1951 new coastal express destinations were added as two routes, one to Margate, Broadstairs and Ramsgate, and the other to Eastbourne and Hastings, all of which would have been considered too far away in pre-war days from Maidenhead. The value of special events drawing large crowds was acknowledged with a special license to operate to the Agricultural Show at Cambridge held between 3rd and 16th July. In fact, as a note to younger readers, the Country took quite a few years to get back to normal, with some foodstuffs still rationed until 1954!

During October 1951 the opportunity was taken to renew the full range of excursions and tours already on the license, whilst also adding a few more, the full list being-

Tour	Destination	Duration
1	Cheddar Gorge	Day
2	Southend-on-Sea	Day
3	Hastings	Day
4	Portsmouth	Day
5	Worthing & Brighton	Day
6	Bognor Regis & Littlehampton	Day
7	Margate, Broadstairs, & Ramsgate	Day
8	Bournemouth	Day
9	Eastbourne	Day
10	Hayling Island	Day
11	Southampton	Day
12	Goodwood (Motor or Horse)	Events
13	Epsom Races	Events
14	Kempton Park Races	Events
15	Hurst Park Races	Events
16	Sandown Races	Events
17	Ascot Races	Events
18	Newbury Races	Events
19	Windsor Races	Events
20	Hampton Court	Half-day
21	Oxford	Various
22	Thame Show	Event
23	Hindhead	Various
24	Aldershot Military Tattoo	Evening
25	Virginia Water	Various
26	Finchampstead	Various
27	London Zoo	Day
28	Finchampstead Ridges	Half-day
29	Thames Ditton	Half-day
30	California-in-England	Various
31	Wallingford circular tour	Half-day
32	Henley circular tour	Half-day
33	Wargrave circular tour	Half-day
34	Hambleden circular tour	Half-day
35	Nettlebed circular tour	Half-day
36	Burnham Beeches & Beaconsfield	Half-day
37	Pinner	Football
38	Berkhampstead	Football
39	Uxbridge	Football
40	Egham	Football
41	Chesham	Football
42	Hounslow	Football
43	Belvedere	Football
44	Braintree	Football
45	Aylesbury	Football
46	Carshalton	Football
47	Edgware Town	Football
48	Slough	Football
49	Walton & Hersham	Football
50	Wembley	Events
51	Sliverstone Motor Circuit	Events

Tour	Destination	Duration
52	Farnborough Air Display	Events
53	Chessington Zoo	Day
54	Harringay Arena	Events
55	Maidstone	Football
56	Grays or Tilbury	Football
57	Eastbourne	Football
58	Worthing	Football
59	Epsom	Football

Additional tours -

Tour	Destination	Duration
60	Lingfield Races	Events
61	Gatwick Races	Events
62	Festival of Britain	Events

19

Note - The half-day tours could be afternoon or the evening, that to Oxford also included theatre events.

Returning to the fleet, there was a need for several more secondhand coaches with higher capacity, which led to the purchase of another two particularly interesting vehicles. The first came in May 1952, though built back in April 1930 as an AEC 'Regal' 662-type (GF 5128). However, its original body had been replaced in 1938 by a new Duple 32-seater front-door coach body, whilst still owned by *Blue Belle Motors* of London. That firm was by then under the control of *Red & White Services*, so after the coaching activity ended due to the war, it moved to that parent fleet, having been fitted with a Gardner 5LW oil engine in 1939. It remained in the fleet until February 1955, after which it passed to a showman. Indeed, Maidenhead-based coaches passing to showman was a recurring theme, largely because of the over-wintering area near The Bear Hotel, which was occupied for many years.

The much travelled 'Regal' seen soon after arrival and painting in the twin-blue livery, at the Avenue Road Coach Park in Bournemouth. Alan Cross found it between two Bedford OB's from the Smith's Luxury Coaches of Reading fleet, and on that occasion it was sporting a radiator evidently taken from a 'Regent'!

The other purchase took place in March 1953, bringing a 1948 Leyland 'Tiger' PS1/1 chassis fitted with 33-seater coach body by Bellhouse & Hartwell of Bolton, so a rarity amongst Southern operators. EBU 790 had originated with *Spencer Tours* of Bury and would stay for over 4 years.

The Bellhouse & Hartwell body on EBU 790 had a largely Burlingham look about it, popular with some Lancashire operators, and at a time when new bodies were hard to come by, and it is shown at Bell Street.

From February 1952 the contract to Northolt was fully detailed to show it was the hire of a 20-seater coach, with a route of Pond House (8.05am) – Castle Hill – The Bear – Maidenhead Bridge – Taplow (Hitcham Road) – Cippenham – Slough (Wellington Street and Chandos Street) – Uxbridge Road (Drill Hall) – Crooked Billet – Stag & Hounds (Church Road) – Northolt Airport (8.55am). The returning journey left at 5.35pm and reached Pond House at 6.25pm, the cost of the coach being £2 and 10 shillings per day.

For May 1952 another pick-up was added on those coastal expresses noted earlier with Holyport etc., with one at Warfield Stores on Warfield Street, whilst the Havant route also called there after Cox Green and Waltham Church.

Opposite, the classic rear-end and side profile of the pre-war style Duple body on GF 5128, seen on a trip to Southsea. The sweeping side flash and stepped waistrail were typical features, but gave it a dated look.

Although not documented as such, the acquisition of a pair of Bedford OB coaches from the fleet of British European Airways was in fact linked to the contract operation on the behalf of its staff to the developing Heathrow Airport. In that fashion, Carters came to own the pair in December 1953 as OMP 141/3, both with Duple 'Vista' 29-seat bodies. OMP 143 is seen in Bell Street in the blue livery and with various coastal express destinations shown on the glass louvres on its sides.

Also bearing the same body on an OB chassis was this example from the Isle of Wight. GDL 14 had been new in April 1949 to the Ventnor-based operator Randall, but like many of the island's coaches, spent most Winters in store, so they were generally a good buy for their apparent age. It is also seen parked near the Bell Street Garage in its blue phase, also with the coastal destinations visible on the side louvres, though the order varied between individual coaches.

GDL 14 had arrived in 1955 and remained until 1960, so this later view at Goodwood Races sees it in the cream, red and blue livery. It has a sticker for Maidenhead to mark it out as a direct run to the town, but other coaches may have worked to there direct from Marlow, Slough or Cookham according to the bookings for that day. The racecourse on the top of the South Downs was quite a spectacular setting for both the horse-racing and the motoring events.

In respect of the express service to Bournemouth, the route took in quite a lot of relatively new housing areas to the west of Maidenhead, as Castle Hill – Pond House – Cox Green – Woodlands Park – Thicket Corner – Littlewick Green (Wheatsheaf) – Knowl Hill (Seven Stars) – Kiln Green (Queen's Head) – Southampton (Royal Pier) – Bournemouth (Avenue Road). From June 1952 a new feeder service brought passengers into Maidenhead for pre-booked coastal express services from Cippenham (Everitts Corner) at 7.45am, whilst that month saw a regular special shuttle service from Maidenhead to the Cox Green Flower Show, a route also shared with *Thames Valley* at common fares of 6d between 2pm and 10pm according to traffic.

August 1952 saw further excursion destinations added, with Boreham for motor-racing, White City Stadium for events and an afternoon or evening tour to the Festival of Britain Pleasure Gardens between the Royal Festival Hall and County Hall on London's South Bank, a legacy of the main event of 1951. From late 1952 the contract with ML Aviation to the White Waltham Airfield was increased to two vehicles at 26 or 33 seats, according to demand, and from December the BEA/BOAC contract first mentions Heathrow as the destination, now calling for a 26 or 32-seater type.

An extra tour was added in late 1952 in readiness for the forthcoming Coronation of Princess Elizabeth in 1953, which ran over the procession route, proving to be a popular afternoon or evening tour, for which a guide joined the coach in London, whilst on some dates there was a firework finale over the River Thames.

However, of lasting significance was a new contract on behalf of the Southern Electricity Board, which had been formed under the Nationalisation of that utility, and its Headquarters was set in the period manor of Woolley Hall, built at Littlewick Green in 1780 and surrounded by 240 acres of landscaped parkland. It was another long-running contract, which set out from the Station at Maidenhead, very handy for the Garage.

Another license held for many years from the pot-war resumption of Pony Racing at Hawthorn Hill saw the firm operating to there from Maidenhead Station on all race days, whilst *Thames Valley* held the license for transfers from Bracknell Station to that venue.

By the 1953 season, only two coach operators were active in the town of Maidenhead, *Carters* with *Alpha Coaches* and the *Hoopers* with its *Three Lilies Coaches*, more about the latter under its own heading of course. Also, still active was *John Chastell* based at Cookham Dean, who had originally been partner in a local bus service, also fully detailed elsewhere in this volume. Later he had continued as *Dean Luxury Coaches*, but by 1954 he wanted to retire, so it was

agreed that *Carters* would take over that operation from after the end of the Summer season in September 1954. In fact, the new owner re-registered the operation as *Dean Luxury Coaches (Maidenhead) Ltd.,* though the address was at No.119 King Street in Maidenhead. With it came a trio of coaches, which were standard for the fleet, other than the fact that *Chastell* tended to have less seats than the usual quota for the Duple 'Vista' body, only 27 instead of 29. They were DJB 117 new to *Dean* in September 1946, FBL 779 also bought new in August 1949 and MPP 658 a December 1949 new to *Lucas (Fifield Garage)* of Slough and later to *Chastell*. All three were retained, plus an order for a new coach for 1955 delivery was earmarked for that fleet, KRX 933, delivered in May as a Bedford SBG with Duple 'Vega' 38-seater coach body.

As already noted on the previous page, another Bedford OB (GDL 14) came from the Isle of White in January 1955, whilst in March of that year another pair of secondhand OB's with standard Duple 'Vista' 29-seater coach bodies joined the fleet as another refugee from the Island as EDL 376, new to *Paul's Tours* of Ryde in 1947, along with KYF 896, a 1950 example from *Barnaby*, London N7. These coaches ousted the last of the Bedford WTB-types from the fleet, and it perhaps should be mentioned that such vehicles usually came via one of the dealers, often Arlingtons of North London or Percy Sleeman of West London, both of whom would at times send prospective purchases down for inspection at Maidenhead, or notify in advance of upcoming withdrawals against new deliveries.

FRX 533 had been bought new in 1950 and ran for the firm until October 1964. At some later point it was given a thorough refurbishment, coming out in this variation of the livery, with red lower area and a blue side flash on a cream background, and was caught by Phil Moth when parked near the Tower of London.

The SBG-type mentioned above was the new larger replacement to bring Bedford in line with maximum dimensions permitted, whilst retaining a petrol engine, the 'G' standing for gasoline, as was the American term for that type of fuel, making it an economical coach.

An order for two SBG's with Duple 'Vega' 41-seat bodies were delivered between November 1956 and March 1957 as LRX 826 and 827, the last coaches to start out in the blue livery. LRX 826 was photographed by the well-known Ray Simpson in his home town of Oxford, as it was parked at Gloucester Green Bus Station in the area reserved for visiting coaches. The 'butterfly' grille on the Duple coach body would grace 1000's of fleet, both large and small, no coach park being complete without one.

Bedford SBG-type coach SUO 826 from the nearside at the races somewhere, the horses having a popular following from the Maidenhead area.

SUO 826 was indeed one of a trio of SBG's purchased in 1958, the other pair being NHO 189/90, both with Duple 'Vega' 38-seater bodies, whereas SUO seated only 36. They came from *Coliseum* of Gosport and had

been new in January 1955, passing to *Carters* in May 1958, followed by SUO in December.

It was soon after then that Bill Nash of Clare Road in Maidenhead joined the firm as a driver. He had joined the Army in 1937, seeing service with the Royal Berkshire Regiment in India and Burma before being demobbed in 1945.

On return he went to drive for *London Transport* at Windsor, alongside his brother Fred. Both duly married their 'clippies', and indeed son Len Nash grew up to be interested in, as he put it, 'anything with wheels or wings'. Bill went over to *Moore's (Imperial BS)* about 1953, but was always inclined to see the next job as looking better, so did other driving jobs with lorries or vans, until going over to *Carters* in 1959. Initially he was put on the heavy half-cabs, 'Lancets' FMO 482/3 or the Foden FJB 406, but after a few months was allocated Bedford OB KYF 896 as his dedicated coach.

The advert as used in the 1960 Kelly's Directory had a classic Burlingham 'Seagull'-bodied coach, though the fleet never actually featured such a vehicle.

Returning to Bill Nash, he now progressed to SB3-type SOU 370, which he christened 'Sue', whilst his mate Bill Ansell had LRX 826, which started a friendly rivalry between the two men. Young Len would go to the garage in school holidays, helping out with checking oil and water levels, though he found the big bonnet on the Foden hard to manage. In return for such help he got free trips on the coastal expresses when they were not full, which gave him opportunities to 'spot' buses, trains and planes where they took him, he recalls the Bournemouth Coach Park as always interesting. But his father only stayed with *Carters* for about two years, then went over to *Bray Transport*, before going back to *Thames Valley* again. Perhaps ironically, his next move was to *Blue Bus* of Slough, as they sold the Windsor to Maidenhead route to the *'Valley'* in 1965, so he ended up back on their books, though kept on his old familiar duty! He stayed on there until 1974, not driving PSV's again after that.

In the meantime, on the licensing front, the BEA run had been altered to start at Pinkneys Green from January 1956, whilst March of that year finally saw the firm granted a license to Weymouth, subject to the conditions required to protect the *Royal Blue* coaches. That was all part of the scramble *by Smith's, Carters* and *Brimblecombe Bros.* to gain a slice of the growing population of Bracknell New Town, which involved some difficult sittings of the Traffic Court, even making the National Press as an unfolding story.

Also, from January 1957, the SEB contract to Woolley Hall rose to 2 vehicles, whilst that same month saw new contracts for ML Aviation at White Waltham Airfield to start from Wokingham (Town Hall) at 7.30 and 8,20am, running by way of Bracknell (High Street) – Warfield Street, whilst the other was from Reading at 7.15 and 8.10 via Sonning – Twyford-Knowl Hill (Seven Stars), all returning at 5.35pm daily.

A further feeder coach had been added from February 1957 starting at Burchetts Green for pre-booked seats on the coastal expresses and excursions.

Further tripartite friction followed the Bournemouth application in October 1956, now re-routed through the New Forest, and much more on those matters will be found in the volume dedicated to Smith's Coaches.

More football-related destinations added from Autumn 1956 were to Dorking and Wembley, with all the International Fixtures attended. Over the Winter of 1956/7 more destinations for excursions were licensed to pick up at Warfield and Bracknell, covering Kew Gardens, Goodwood (motor and horse events), the Air Display at Farnborough, Aldershot Military Tattoo, and a Hindhead tour, as well as approval for the expresses to Bognor Regis & Littlehampton, Worthing & Brighton and Portsmouth, all helping attract more bums-on-seats from the growing Newtowners.

A completely new area of work planned for 1958 was extended tours, with the Blackpool Tour now designated No.1, but joined by No.2 to Eire via the ferry from Holyhead. However, all Maidenhead pick ups now left from Bell Street, as King Street was getting rather congested for such activities. Additional excursions for 1958 were Gatwick Airport, Swanage and Milford-on-Sea,and from 1960 the feeder coach from Marlow started from The Bridge rather than Quoiting Square, which reduced the mileage, whilst Hayling Island was added to the Warfield pick-ups.

SBL 265 was new in March 1959, as a Bedford SB3 with with 41-seater Plaxton 'Consort MkIV'-style body, caught here at the very popular Hayling Island.

A trio of secondhand Duple-bodied Bedfords were added in May 1959 to boost the contract fleet, with a 1949 OB as FBL 756 with 'Vista' 29-seater body new to *Stevens* of Wantage, and the others were both SBG-types with 'Vega' 36-seater bodies as TKO 665 from *Parker* of London NW9 and GGV 822 from another *Carter* at Kentford, both new in 1954. They were followed by SUO 370 mentioned a little earlier, during October 1959, new in 1958 *to Super* of Upminster.

1960 saw a new coach as URX 793, a Bedford SB1-type with Burlingham 'Seagull 60' 41-seater body, and shortly after it arrived in May it was hired by HM The Queen to transport Commonwealth Prime Ministers to a lunch at The Hinds Head in Bray, adorned with the Royal Cipher.

A nice one-year old coach added in July 1960 was VOT 507, a Bedford SB1-type with 41-seater Duple 'Vega' body, new to Super of Upminster. It was fitted with the 'printer's cap' Perspex shade over the front dome, and optional extra available in clear, blue, green or orange, popular with some operators. It is shown here parked on a bomb-site near Waterloo Station. The drivers prided themselves on knowing the best spots to park, cheap and preferably near a good café!

A notable withdrawal in 1963 was the last half-cab coach in service with the firm, Dennis 'Lancet' J3-type FMO 483 **seen below**, one of a pair which had served since being purchased new in 1950 and carrying a 35-seater body by Yeates of Loughborough, who were also a Dennis Agent for many years.

Earlier we heard of the taxi service and the provision of funeral cars, the original types in use being Charron and Renault, though Morris cars were favoured for taxis from the 1930's. Although there are few details of those vehicles, an early motor-hearse was based on another Crossley X-type, though certainly not one identified for use with living passengers! Funeral work ceased in

1967, but the taxis continued, with 7 licenses held, though reducing to just 1 by 1977, which in fact was hired out to Bernie, who drove coaches part-time as well, spending the rest of the day on the Station taxi rank. Both types of vehicle had for some years been garaged in a lean-to shed behind the King Street premises, though the access was from Bell Street, opposite the coach garage.

The *Dean Coaches* fleet ran in the same livery as the main fleet, with the inherited FBL 779 and MPP 658, along with the new delivery KRX 933, but when a pair of Bedford SBG's came in 1958 as NHO 189/90, the latter was allocated to *the Dean* fleet, both having 38-seater Duple 'Vega' bodies and new to Coliseum of Gosport, nice clean coaches from the dealer Baker's.

The above additions, both new and secondhand, saw a bit of a clear-out of older classic types, with 1958 seeing the departure of a 1945 Bedford OWB as CRX 648 and Bedford OB OMP 141, one of the pair acquired from *British European Airways* in association with the staff contract. During 1959 OB-type OMP 143 went, along with the 1948 Maudslay 'Marathon MkIII' HOM 903. They were followed during 1960 by Bedford OB DJB 410, bought new in 1946, and secondhand scquired examples EDL 376 and GDL 14, as well as Duple-bodied SB-series coaches LRX 826 and GGV 822. 1961 saw the sale of only one of the 1950 Yeates-bodied Dennis 'Lancet J3'-types as FMO 482, whilst 1962 saw the disposal of the Wadham-bodied Foden PVSV6 coach FJB 406, a vehicle unique in the area, and quite a rarity on the national scene. A colourised representation of it in the cream, red and blue livery is used on the front cover of this volume., there being no colour photos from that era, and the author admits he never took any photos of the fleet himself!

LRX 826 was one of a pair bought new in late 1956 and early 1957, both on Bedford SBG chassis and carrying Duple 'Vega' 41-seater bodies, with the new 'Butterfly' grille'.When new they wore the two-tone blue livery, but it is seen when repainted into the pale cream, red and blue scheme, which suited the moulding lines on that design nicely. At that time the fleetname was still Alpha, set in the device seen on the body sides.

The Bedford VAL was a concept to provide a 36-foot-long coach and 52-seater capacity within the legal framework relating to current axle loadings. The wheels were all of 17 inches, with a twin-steer at the front, not an entirely new concept, as some 1930's Leyland chassis had used the same idea. Carters only took this one example as 849 EBL, fitted with a Plaxton 'Panorama' body and delivered in June 1963. Despite running for over 12 years, no further examples of that type were ordered or added as secondhand purchases. Note that it is lettered Carters rather than Alpha, in reflection of the now wider involvement with travel of all kinds through the Travel Agency.

Other secondhand additions in 1961-2 had all been Bedford SB-types, though with varied coachwork. SBG-type NHO 600 came from *Darvill* at Watford, with Duple 'Vega' 36-seater body new in 1955, SB1-type XOR 904 had a Plaxton 'Embassy' 41-seater body new in 1960 and from *Super* of Upminster again, and SB1's GEF 203/4 were a pair of 41-seaters with Plaxton 'Consort' MkIV bodies new in 1959 to *Beeline* of West Hartlepool.

Another longstanding contract involved the presence of a number of United States Air Force families in the area, whose children went to a dedicated school nearby. Other local school contracts followed but details are mostly lacking for the period 1946 to 1960.

Ask any old coach driver about what he liked about the job, and two things are to the fore. Firstly, the sense of being largely in charge of your day, unlike factory or office work, but also those amusing incidents that made up for the more mundane days. Bill Nash recalled two such incidents, as his son Len reminded me. On one private hire a party of OAP's went to visit White Horse Hill at Uffington, but most passengers did not fancy the climb up to the summit of the hill-fort, so Bill did a cross-country route to bring 'Sue' onto the top level, probably the only such incident of a coach there, before the era of the New Age Travellers that is. After a look round, most needed a loo break, but there were no facilities there (or at the base car park), so the gents went to the scarce bushes, but that left the ladies in distress. So, Bill pulled up the inspection panels in the centre aisle, the ladies lining up to pee through the floor! They were so happy he got a good tip that day.

On another trip to the coast, the coach encountered a tail-back at the Jolly Farmer roundabout between Bagshot and Camberley, but one passenger said he knew a short-cut, so Bill followed his directions, which saw the coach rambling on for about 45 minutes, until fetching up in a parkland area of well-kept grounds, coming to some large ornate gates, only to escorted out by armed sentries from the Royal Military Academy at Sandhurst, just a few miles further down the A30!

Returning to the sequence of events, the business was added to as a Travel Agency in 1963, with the same address in King Street, and a branch at No.2 Market Street in the town centre. Apart from dealing with the coach bookings, a wide range of services were available, with worldwide and business travel. It was an aspect of the business under the guidance of third generation Fred Carter (born 1931), whilst his brother Bob (born 1937) looked after the coaching side, with assistance from their sister Beryl Green (1934) in the office. The Travel Agency would steadily expand with further branches in Marlow and even Reading. In line with that activity it was probably inevitable that the firm would duly consider operating its own extended tours to Continental Europe, as we shall see soon.

The funeral car hire was still active, and at times the coach drivers might act as pall-bearers or drivers, as a useful supplement to their income especially in the quiet months for coaching. At around 1960 there was a Daimler hearse, along with a pair of Austin 'Sheerliner' limousines, which were housed in a lean-to behind the King Street offices, and were hired out to the local undertakers, but that all ceased during 1967.

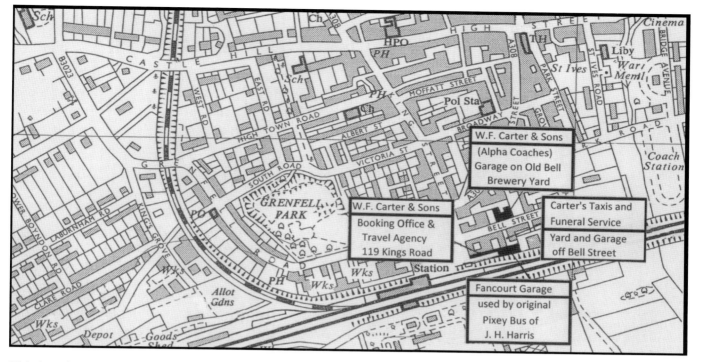

This location map shows the town in the mid-1960's, with the Railway Station bottom centre. Adjacent to the up line is the yard of The Fancourt Garage, where several earlier operators based their vehicles, close-by to the entrance for No119 King Street, Carter's Booking Office and in due course Travel Agency. The yard behind can be seen with its access from Bell Street, whilst on the north of Bell Street can be seen the coach garage and parking areas, which had expanded in place of several other motor garage firms.

Another long-standing commitment for Carters involved the practise of Swan-Upping, the checking and marking of Mute Swans along The River Thames on behalf of The Queen, The Master Swan-Upper and his assistants patrolling the river between Sunbury Lock and Abingdon Bridge each July. The job had been covered since 1936, so in 1986 a Royal Warrant was issued to the firm on completion of 50 years' service. The men were based at The Thames Hotel in Maidenhead, travelling out each day to the stretch of river under review, then the driver was told which pub to collect them from that evening. They were invariably well-oiled by then, plus some were still wet from misadventures during the day!

Added in 1964 were 188 CUY an SB1-type Bedford with Plaxton 'Embassy' body seating 41, and 932 DLK, a Duple 'Bella Vista' b29-seater body on a VAS1 chassis. The latter had been new in 1962 to *Lewis* of Farnborough.

Their arrival ousted Bedford OB's FBL 756 and FRX 533, there being a general requirement for higher capacities, as the post-war 'baby boomers reached Secondary School age. Only one coach arrived in 1965 as OCR 337, a 1955 Bedford SBG with Duple 'Vega' 36-seater body, new to *Summerbee* of Southampton. Outgoing were a further pair of OB-types as FBL 779 and MPP 658, the last examples in both the *Alpha* and *Dean* fleets in fact. The latter name was only represented by KRX 933 an SBG new in 1955.

Plaxton-bodied 188 CUY was caught at Hastings on a coastal express, so carries an on-hire sticker to conform with the licensing agreement with Southdown Motor Services. It had been new to Supreme of Stourbridge.

Quite a few changes occurred to the fleet in 1966, with Bedfords SUO 826, OCR 337 and VOT 507 all being disposed of. The incoming coaches were a mix of used and new, with ACE 164B and 939 ECE as Bedford SB5's both with Duple 'Bella Vega' 41-seater bodies new in 1964 to Cambridge operators. Bought new were a pair of Bedford VAM5's with Plaxton 'Panorama' bodies seating 45 as JRX 48/9D. There were no additions to the fleet during 1967, but 1968/9 saw a quartet of Bedford SB5-types acquired, but not all alike. CJU 578B was new in 1964 to *King* of

Amersham., and it had a 41-seater Plaxton 'Embassy' body, whereas 4020AW, 4593 MU and 23 JTM all had Duple 'Bella Vega' bodies also seating 41.

*4020 AW had been new to Whittle of Highley, in whose livery it is seen **above,** they also used red, cream and blue, but not in the same proportions as Carters whilst **below** we have the other side of that body type as 23 JTM with Buckmaster of Leighton Buzzard.*

Outgoing coaches were GEF 203 and possibly NHO 190 and NHO 600, which is shown opposite. 6593 MU and 23 JTM ousted Bedford SBG-types LRX 827 and KRX 933, both originally purchased new, the latter being the last to carry the *Dean Coaches* fleetname. The name had been retained due to the considerable goodwill that had come with that acquisition. 1970 saw no coaches added, but quite a clear-out took place, with Bedford SB-types GEF 204, SBL 265 and URX 793 all going, along with the 29-seater VAS1 932 DLK. Most, if not all, passed through the dealer Baker of Farnham, often as a part-exchange on his sale stock, his showroom always worth a visit if passing that way.

NHO 600 carries the cream, red and blue livery as applied to the Duple 'Vega'-style bodies, the blue forming the darker area on the side-stripe.

On the 'Bella Vega' bodies, passengers would often make for the front nearside seats for the good view, but if the sun came out, that could be a rather hot place!

Loadings on some of the school and works contracts had increased, so in 1971 a secondhand Bedford VAM70 was added as PUW 33F, one of a number with Duple 'Viceroy' 45-seater bodies new to Bexleyheath Transport in 1968.

The higher capacity was also useful on the express services, so here we have PUW 33F at Southsea.

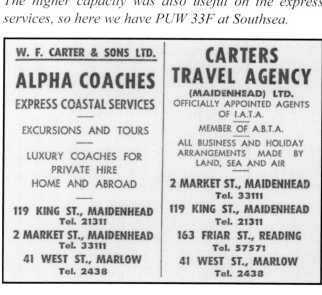

One of the school contracts also now needed more seats, leading to the purchase of the first, and indeed only, double-decker operated by Carters. 411 COR was a Dennis 'Loline MkIII', new in 1962 to Aldershot & District as No.411. As that operator had recently merged with Thames Valley to form Alder Valley, it had received the poppy red and white livery, which it retained whilst with Carters.

The 'Loline' was a licensed version of the Bristol 'Lodekka' built at Guildford by Dennis, so Aldershot & District had several batches. This type featured a 68-seater body by Alexander, the front sliding door being controlled by the driver. Carters made use of the front destination screens for the permanent display shown.

The outgoing coaches of 1972 were both Bedford SB-types with Duple 'Vega' bodies as LRX 826 and SUO 370, whilst 1973 saw two Plaxton-bodied examples go

as XOR 904 and 188 CUY. Apart from the double-decker, 1972 also saw a pair of Bedford VAM14's acquired from the Grey-Green fleet as JUV 525/6D, both new in 1966 with Duple 'Bella Venture, bodies seating 45.

The first of many coaches coming to Maidenhead after service with the George Ewer Group fleets, which included Grey-Green and Orange Luxury Coaches.

The coaches obtained from Grey-Green were found to be most worthwhile, being well-maintained by that long-established North London operator. It had an extensive network of express services, mostly to coastal destinations along the South Coast, Kent and East Anglia, built up over the decades by London area and other acquisitions. JUV 526D is seen here repainted in the cream, red and blue livery on a school job.

The VAMs delivered to Ewer in 1967 had the improved 'Viceroy'-style body, seen here on NMU 552E, one of two passing to Carters in 1973. Although mainly used on contracts, they also got to the coast on a regular basis, as in this sunny view. Both remained with the firm until 1980 and were liked by the drivers, but received this cream and red version of the livery.

Jeff Jones caught NMU 559E parked in the Bell Street yard, which by the 1970's had been expanded to take account of the larger coaches now in use, a far cry from the 29-seater Bedford OB's of earlier times. Note that the side lettering is as Carters and no Alpha now in use, having disappeared from the newspaper adverts back in 1967. As it was also used by several other operators, certain vehicles have, over the years, been erroneously noted as belonging to the Maidenhead concern, or appear in photo selections, but see the Fleet List on pages 93-94 for a full list of those actually operated.

Another coach purchased from Grey-Green was this Bedford VAM70 as VLF 37G, though it had been new to Birch Bros., another old-established North London operator based at Kentish Town. It carried a Plaxton 'Panorama Elite' body seating 45 and was new in 1969, coming to the fleet in 1973. It also gained a cream and red livery, and is seen on a race day excursion.

Mention has been made of the livery change and its origins, as Bob Carter so liked the look of the pair of coaches obtained from the high-class tour specialist operator Pleasureways of Altrincham in 1974. They were Bedford VAM70's with Plaxton 'Panorama Elite' 45-seater bodies, one of which was HTU 93G. They were the only coaches fitted with Telmar Rretarders, useful on tours where sustained braking was required. The centre of the bodies were in an ochre shade of yellow

Looking quite like several other recent purchases, former Grey-Green YYX 591H was in fact a Bristol LHL6L chassis, with 51-seater Plazton 'Panorama Elite' body, which came to Carters in 1976, but only stayed for a year. It is seen with original operator Grey-Green, the chassis type enjoying popularity at the time, mostly with coach operators.

Jeff Jones took this photo of HTU 93G in the Bell Street yard. The lettering was in red with shading and looked good on the ochre background, these coaches also bringing an enhanced level of comfort for the longer tours now being advertised.

We will now benefit from Jeff's recollections of the operations during the period 1977 to 1989, when he drove for the firm.

The main daily contract operation focussed on the Brylcream factory, manufacturing hair-oil south-west of the town centre at Norreys Drive.3 coaches came in from Reading, and one each from Bracknell, Windsor and Slough. That later reduced to just 2 from Reading, whilst the Windsor and Slough was combined. That from Bracknell only later warranted a minibus, driven by a part-timer Bernie, who spent the rest of the day as driver of the taxi, whose license he hired from Carters, so when numbers got down to just a couple, he used the car instead. One of the coaches ran on from the Brylcream factory to cover a contract to the Rank Film Studios at nearby Denham. The Beecham's factory at Slough was also served from the High Wycombe area, so if short of coaches, Carters would hire-in to cover that.

Royal Ascot Race Week saw coaches used to ferry in additional Police Officers, and Jeff recalls that no bad how the traffic got, the coaches were always waived through by officers on point-duty! That also led to several coaches going North during the Miner's Strike of 1984/5, taking officers drafted in from Berkshire and Buckinghamshire, or occasionally non-striking miners.

The school contracts were the other mainstay of daily operations, with 3 for the Blue Coat School at Sonning, collecting over a wide area, whilst for the Education Authority there were a trio of schools covered. The run started at Knowl Hill, then across to Hurley, slong the back-road to Bisham, before running back into town past Furze Platt School, then onto Altwood and finally the Grammar School. In respect of the latter, the assignments got down to just one, so if he was known not to be attending, the Bisham pick up could be

omitted, though that school also hired a coach for Saturday fixtures for the rugby season.

The other school covered was St. Joseph's RC, situated in Shaggy Calf Lane on the edge of Slough. One ran from the western housing estates of Slough, whereas the other ran from Langley. There were also worker's contracts to the Mars factories at Liverpool Road and Dundee Road, interworked with the St. Joseph runs, though during school holidays minibuses would suffice.

Carters were the stand-by operator when trains failed on the Maidenhead to Marlow Branch, which was quite a regular occurance.

The express services had long-established feeder coaches, so when Carters heard that *Jeffways* of High Wycombe were ceasing such operations, from its driver Dave Edwards, who happened to live in 'Wycombe, they arranged for him to take a coach home to cover that additional run, which was YDF at the time.

Jeff took these photos of Ford 'Transit' minibus VTP 879L, as in fact the minibuses are rare in photos. It is parked in the lay-by by the café at Knowl Hill, with the Seven Stars pub in the background. Note the mix of Alpha and Carters fleetnames still being carried. The livery was an adaption of the ochre and white used on the larger vehicles.

Both of the former Grey-Green YRQ's PGM 646/7L were on the same Derby Day excursion in this Phil Moth photo.

Incoming vehicles for 1977 were the above minibus, which had a 12-seater body by Robin Hood of Fareham, plus a trio of full-size coaches all being on Bedfords, PGM 646/7L as YRQ's with Plaxton 'Panorama Elite MkIII' 45-seater bodies , new in 1973 to *Grey-Green*. The third was a YRT-type with 53-seater Plaxton 'Supreme' bodywork as former *Bexleyheath Transport* HMV 643N of 1975. Their arrival ousted VAM14-type JUV 526D and the solitary Bristol LHL6L YYX 591H.

HMV 643N was also at Epsom, one of about 6 coaches there on that popular occasion.

1978 saw several nice coaches added, with VKM 963J being a1970 Bedford VAM70 carrying a Plaxton 'Panorama Elite MkII body seating 45 and new to *Sonner* of Chatham. The was MUL 700P, an 11-metre long YMT-type with 53-seater Duple 'Dominant' body new in 1976 to The *Ewer Group* once again.

The operation of the Travel Agencies was largely down to Fred Carter, whilst Bob looked after the coach side. He had developed a good relationship with the Ewer Management, who would inform him when coaches were available for sale, then he (and a driver) would travel up by train and return with their choices. Fred, incidentally, had appeared on the telly in an early form of Travel Show, plus he was also responsible for the development of the extended tours, which duly included continental destinations, his knowledge largely derived from the bookings he had handled as agent for various other operators, so we shall look at those developments next.

The original extended tours had been to Blackpool, for the popular period of the illuminations, which started back in 1958 and ran for over 25 years.along with the Flower Festival at Spalding in Lincolnshire. The popularity of that led to a similarly-themed tour to Holland, which first ran in May 1981, and included the famous displays of the Keukenhof Gardens, a visit to a Cheese Market and Amsterdam Canal Cruise. As it was based in the coastal resort of Scheviengen, it had the bonus of sandy beaches and its modern pier, that trip being repeated for many years.Next came a Paris and Rheims break, with guided city tour and a Champagne-tasting. A number of short-breaks ran to Jersey or Guernsey, making use of the faster ferries, some on the Sealink 'Jazz Boat, whilst the French Coast and Duty-Free hypermarkets featured regularly, using the large Hovercraft then in service. Pressing further into Europe was a 'Rhine In Flames 'tour, Caen & the Normandy Beaches, also the Belgian Ardennes and the Weiz Beer Festival, whilst by using the DFDS Line 'floating hotels', a mini-cruise to Sweden and another to Hamburg featured, the furthest destination reached was Lake Molveno, on the edge of The Dolomites, including tours to Verona, Venice and Lake Garda. Bob didn't trust a Bedford for that, so hired a coach from *Hodges Coaches* of Sandhurst on that occasion!

MUL 700P Was the 11-metre version of the Bedford YMT chassis, and the coach is also seen at the Derby. Its driver had found there were letters in the destination boxes, so has set CCL for Carters Coaches Ltd.

Apart from the continental developments, a good selection of home-based tours was offered each year Amongst those were North or West Wales, the Edinburgh Tattoo, The Lake District, Herriott Country in Yorkshire, along with Derbyshire, Northumberland and Devon, both North and South, as well as Cornwall.

It may be recalled that back in the 1950's Carters had been one of the operators embroiled in a difficult case through the Traffic Court, which also *involved Smith's* of Reading. Whilst it was true that some of the arguments centred on who should serve the growing population of Bracknell New Town, it was also the objections raised by certain operators based on the coast that presented difficulties to a number of applicants, their objections focussing on abstraction from their licensed services. In the end the Traffic Commissioner had brokered an agreement, whereby such objections would be removed if the operators wishing to serve those points paid an annual fee. In that way *Carters* (and others) had been able to add direct bookings to a number of additional points on the coastal express services, with the Eastbourne and Hastings service gaining access to points east of Brighton, through agreement with *Southdown Motor Services,* which added Rottingdean, Seaford, Peacehaven, Newhaven and Bexhill-on-Sea, whilst from Chichester they could reach The Witterings, Bracklesham Bay and Selsey Bill.

A similar situation existed west of Bournemouth, whereby agreement with *Southern & Western Nationals* (as proprietors of *Royal Blue*), allowed the coaches to reach Weymouth, Wool and Wareham. In each case the coaches operated technically on hire to

those concerns, and that arrangement continued through to August 1978.

PGM 646L at Epsom for The Derby. All Grey-Green coaches had route number blinds, used in this case to identify No.2 coach within the large crowd, whereas VKM 963J has a paper stickerNo.4 in the windscreen.

1980 saw the departure of a trio of Bedford VAM-types as PUW 33F and NMU 552/9E.

YDF 295K had arrived with its cream paintwork in fine order, so it was not repainted for several years, seen in another Derby Day photo by Phil Moth. It had been new in 1979 to Perrett of Shipton Oliffe. The incoming coaches for 1979 were both Bedfords, but YDF 295K was a Bedford YRQ with Plaxton 'Panorama Elite MkII' body seating 45, whereas SYU 726S was s YMT with Duple 'Dominant MkII 53-seater body, new to Grey-Green in 1977.

SYU 726S is lettered Carters Continental Tours.

Further coaches from *Grey-Green* followed as Duple 'Dominant MkII-bodied Bedford YMT's RYL 718/29R, YYK 743T and YYL 781/4T in 1981-5, then the final coach purchased reflected the requirements of longer tours, being a Volvo B58-61 carrying a Plaxton 'Supreme 49-seater body fitted with an on-board toilet, as 6 SVK arrived in February 1986, seen opposite.

After using the same Booking Office address for many years, continuing re-development in piecemeal fashion of the town centre resulted in a move to a shop unit at No.91 King Street,,but with the opening of the Nicholson's Walk shopping precinct, both the town centre offices closed in favour of taking No.30 there, just inside from King Street and opposite The Rose pub. However, with other changes afoot, enquiries were directed from late April 1988 to the Bell Street Garage. Indeed, the developers now eyed up that site as

well, so the family found a tempting offer being made, whilst the Council took the view that it preferred the old mix of cottages and industrial uses swept away, so resistance became futile, most of the shareholders now advancing in years.

The Volvo 'Eurocruiser' 6 SVK was duly named Miss Holland and re-registered as YEC 21W.

As of course often happens in such situations, there was not a unanimous view, and whilst Fred Carter was happy to retire, Bob was 6 years his junior and wished to continue with the coach business, so he therefore decided to merge with *Malcom D,ouglas* of Windsor (*MD Coaches*), with the transfer of MUL 700P, RYL 718P, SYU 726S and XYK 743T, under the title *Carters Coaches Ltd.*, initially based in Windsor. But later to a yard near the Horlicks factory at Slough, *MD* having commenced in 1973. Bell Street was vacated by the end of April 1989 and an era was truly ended.

Above, back to the beginning, the original Crossley chara inherited from Stanley Collins (BL 8538) seen outside The Reform pub and sharing a party with Thames Valley Harrington-bodied Thornycroft Car 3 (DP 2130) circa 1924. Local operators often worked together to cope with the larger outings by work's employees or social clubs, so common in those days.

Below – a developer's eye-view of Bell Street and surrounds. The coach garage can be seen in the centre right, with added yard areas, whilst in the lower foreground is the railway land, whilst on the left is the Clock Tower on the Station Approach. Re-development also affected Queen Street at the top of the picture. The large repository to the right of the coach garage had been there many years, whilst at the far end of Bell Street was the ground of Maidenhead United Football Club.

John Charles Chastell
Douglas Gordon Gray
Dean Bus Service/Dean Luxury Coaches
Cookham Dean, Berkshire

John Chastell had been born at No12. Moon Street in the North London area of Islington in December 1889, though his father had originated from Reading. By 1911 he was still living at home, but now located at No.97 Cloudesley Road in Barnsbury, also North London, employed as a private chauffeur. He married Nora Ramsden in February 1914, and by the time their daughter Dorothy was born in January 1915 they had re-located to Cookham Dean, where he was chauffeur to the local Dr. Basil Lawrence of Dial Close.

He duly served with the Royal Flying Corps from early 1917, returning to the area in due course. According to a local source, he then started a bus service soon after his return, but that cannot be substantiated, so that claim must therefore be treated with some caution.

Certainly, the service is evidenced by the registration of a brand-new Chevrolet LP-type, supplied and bodied as a red-and-maroon painted 14-seater by REAL of Ealing, which as RX 3773 took to the road on 14th February 1929. At that point the Chastells were living at Dial Close Gardens, though as a business address they used the nearby Chequers Inn, at which in due course the landlord Jim Wigginton became the booking agent. The bus was parked next door, but by 1931 the little fleet was kept in the shed then known as The Chequers Garage.

The name Cookham perhaps requires some further comment, as within that area were a number of small settlements as Cookham Village, Cookham Rise and Cookham Dean, the local term 'The 3 Cookhams' used to cover them collectively. It was due to the spread-out nature of that area that a number of small independents sprang up to serve their specific localites.

And, so it was that the *Dean Bus Service* linked that area with Maidenhead, the route taken being Chequers Inn – Cookham Rise (Whyteladyes Lane) – Cookham (Station) – North Town (Harrow Inn) – Maidenhead (Market Street) – Maidenhead (Station), which gave a useful local service, plus linking to the local station and the mainline at Maidenhead. The frequency was hourly and the journey time was 18 minutes each way, but the journeys were so arranged to get passengers into town for 9am, whilst on Saturdays an extra bus at 6.45pm catered for those out shopping and football matches. As was typical of that period, no services ran on Sundays until 2pm, but throughout the week the final journey home was timed for the Rialto Cinema performance.

The fares charged for single journeys were from The Chequers Inn to Cookham Station 2d, to North Town at 5d and into Maidenhead for 6d, plus there was a full journey return fare of 9d.

The second Chevrolet seen as new before registration.

The first Chevrolet was evidently a sound buy, and for May 1929 a similar bus was ordered from the same coachworks, which entered service on 13th May 1929 as RX 4500. Whereas the original bus had the 4-cylinder engine, this was an LQ-type with 6-cylinder overhead-valve engine.

At the same juncture, a partner joined *John Chastell* as *Douglas Gordon Gray*. He had been born in 1891 in Hackney, but by 1911 he was living in Islington nearby to Chastell, so it seems likely they had kept in touch? He had been a builder's clerk at that point, but during the Great War gained experience as a driver in the Royal Field Artillery.

As already noted, the bus service could be handled by one vehicle, so adverts soon appeared with excursions using the new saloon bus, and also that it was available for private hire. There was, of course, no actual coach operator in the villages, and a trip to the seaside in one of the speedy little Chevies would be as comfortable as any coach. There were also a number of annual events, such as Ascot Races, Henley Regatta and The Derby at Epsom, as well as the Thame Show and the Aldershot Military Tattoo, all now as advertised excursions.

With widened business, it was deemed worthwhile to acquire a secondhand Chevrolet as a back-up vehicle, so an October 1928 LR-type 14-seater bus was bought in 1930, being UR 1444 as new to *E.A. Fenchell* of Enfield, Middlesex. The trio of little Chevies remained at The Chequers Garage, but the business address was switched to the Chastell's new residence at 'Strathsay' in the Dean.

In the meantime, the 1930 Road Traffic Act did not adversely affect the *Dean Bus Service* and its operation, the necessary Road Service Licenses being applied for in April 1931, covering the bus service and also a group of excursions and tours. The latter also called at No.10 Market Street in Maidenhead, a bus stop for the service, where Callingham the tobacconist now served as a booking agent. There were full-day outings to Bognor Regis, Bournemouth, Brighton, Cheddar & Wells, London, Southsea and Worthing, along with outings for racegoers at Ascot, Epsom and Goodwood, the Thame Show and the Aldershot Military Tattoo, the latter an evening trip. Half-day excursions travelled to Beaconsfield & Burnham Beeches, Hampton Court, Henley, High Wycombe, Hindhead, Leith Hill, Newlands Corner, Oxford, Reading, Slough and a tour via Windsor to Virginia Water. For Henley Regatta a frequent bus service was operated with the spare buses on a 2s6d fare, which other operators also offered.

The 1930 Act did, however, change the relationship between the large territorial operators and the independents, whereby the Road Service License held a value when discussing a possible purchase, whilst in the case of *Thames Valley*, it was also the injection of finance by the *Great Western Railway*, which gave it the opportunity to exercise cheque-book diplomacy to reduce the competition. Locally, the *'Valley* had taken over the *Lower Road Bus Service* from *Bert Cowley* in October 1931, whilst its subsidiary *Marlow & District* was being brought under closer control. Although the latter did not serve the Cookhams, its services reached North Town, Furze Platt and Pinkneys Green, so the *'Valley* saw the possibilities of re-organising its routes north of Maidenhead to a more economic pattern.

Indeed, one of its Inspectors had undertaken a roadside survey of loadings during March 1932, so the Traffic & Relations Committee had started to look at buying out the other Cookham-based operators. It approached *Chastell & Gray* in early May with an offer of £2000, actually just for the bus service, as it certainly did not need any small non-standard buses at that time, so that was accepted with effect from 27th May 1933.

With the bus service sold, the partners continued with the hire work and excursions, though the original LP-type bus (RX 3773) was sold straightaway, and in October 1933 the stand-by LP-type Chevrolet (UR 1444) was offered for sale in Commercial Motor, finding a new operator at Stornoway on the Island of Lewis! The newer LQ-type remained with what now became *Dean Luxury Coaches* until sold in June 1934, s new 20-seater Bedford WLB (AME 707) arriving about May 1933.

The small fleet was then engaged on war-related works contracts until peace returned, but on 13th April 1940 the partnership was dissolved by mutual consent, with *Douglas Gray* departing to marry outside the area in 1941, and *John Chastell* continuing as sole owner.

The livery adopted for the coaches from the mid-1930's was one of deep royal blue, but the chance to replace the older stock came in the usual mixed fashion of the early post-war period, with some older types bought for use on contracts, plus some new purchases subject to availability. A new Bedford OB-type came as DJB 117 in September 1946 with Duple 'Vista' 27-seater body, followed by earlier Bedford types as FS 8597 on a WLB chassis with Burlingham 20-seater body dating from May 1934 and WTB-type GRE 987 of July 1938 acquired in November 1948. Those were joined by another new OB with the same bodywork in August 1949 as FBL 779. In September 1950 a similar coach was obtained secondhand as MPP 658, new in only December 1949. The final coach to enter service under the *Dean* name was KRX 333 in May 1955, a Bedford SB-type with Duple 'Vega' 38-seater body. With its arrival the OB DJB 117 was sold on, but withdrawals for the other earlier post-war coaches are not recorded.

In the meantime, two significant events had occurred. The first was a schooldays-only contract, which ran as Cookham Rise (Lower Road off-license) – Cookham Rise (Station) – Cookham Rise (Common Bridge Estate) – Cookham Rise (Harris's Stores) – Cookham Rise (Whyteladyes Lane) – Cookham Dean Junior School. Although arranged by the County Education Authority, it was the responsibility of parents to pay for the termly passes.

The other saw *John Chastell* considering his retirement, so he sold the business to *W. F. Carter & Sons* after the end of the season in September 1954, who re-registered it as *Dean Luxury Coaches (Maidenhead) Ltd.*, with the Registered Office at their HQ at No.119 King Street, though the separate fleet identity was retained for some years. Links were also put in place for the Cookham area passengers to join the coastal express services at Maidenhead, whilst KRX 333 as noted above had that fleetname from new.

Nora Chastell passed away in 1976, followed by John in 1977 at the age of 87.

This photo of RX 4500 was used in adverts by REAL to illustrate it distinctive style of bodywork on that and other chassis of similar capacity by Dennis and Reo, all selling well to independents locally.

Archibald Harry Clinch
Maidonian Allweather Coaches
Maidonian Motor Coaches
Maidonian Bus Services
Maidenhead, Berkshire

Later known as Harry and born at Warborough in Oxfordshire in 1898, we first come across *Archibald Harry Clinch* living with his parents in 1911 at Park House in Warborough, some 3.5 miles north of Wallingford and where his father was employed as a gardener. He followed his father into that line of work and his employer in 1914 was Colonel Dyke. In June 1914 he volunteered for the army and was placed on home service with the 4th Royal Berks Regiment, but after 298 days service he was discharged as medically unfit for war service, returning to civilian life in March 1915.

He duly relocated to live with his sister at Shillingford, just a mile south of Warborough and also in Oxfordshire, giving her Henfield View address when he joined the expanding *British Automobile Traction* Reading Branch in December 1918. However, the post-war route developments were quite rapid, and by June 1919 he was living in Maidenhead at No.42 Grenfell Road, an address often used as lodgings by newly recruited bus crews of that operator. By the following June he was living at 'Fairlight' on the Windsor Road, his employers becoming the *Thames Valley Traction Co. Ltd.* during the following month.

During 1920 *Harry* had married Frances Field at Chertsey in Surrey, and they had moved again by June 1922 to 'Lynfield' on the Windsor Road, but one year later he went further south of the town to No.1 Copse Field Villas at Touchen End on the Holyport to Bracknell road. During these years he drove buses on the service routes, as well as undertaking charabanc work with the Company's Thornycroft J-types.

His first vehicle was a former Great War Talbot, fitted with a 14-seater charabanc body built by Duple Motor Bodies in March 1928, though the registration is not known. He took much of trade from his home area around Holyport, extending out to Winkfield, Warfield and Bracknell, none of which then had dedicated operators of that type.

The first known newspaper advert came in March 1928, by which time he had moved again to No.10 The Council Cottages, Windsor Road in Maidenhead, close to the junction with Shoppenhangers Road. He was using the title *Maidonian Allweather Coaches,* from which it is gleaned more than one vehicle was in use, but fuller details are unfortunately lacking, other than that an advert of September 1931 shows he was then disposing of the Talbot at that point. However, the '30s saw so many good secondhand coaches to be had.

During March 1928 his adverts noted that he was running to the popular Point-to-Point Races held at the Army Remount Deport at Arborfield, some 4.5 miles south of Wokingham in Berkshire, the event in this case being held on Tuesday 27th and for a fare of 3 shillings 6 pence. Other excursions, both locally and to the South Coast were advertised throughout the season until October, and the coaches left from No.57 Queen Street, Maidenhead, where tobacconist Mr. Bryant also served as the booking agent (see map page 92). Other destinations for that season included Bournemouth, Bognor Regis, Brighton, Hindhead, London Zoo, Ramsgate, Southsea, Thame Show and Worthing.

In May 1929 the first new vehicle known to have been purchased by *Harry Clinch* arrived as Chevrolet LQ-type RX 4673, and it carried a 14-seater allweather coach body finished in red and black. From that point on the adverts referred to *Maidonian Motor Coaches.*

Another LQ-type followed in January 1930 as RX 5946, though this time bearing a 14-seater front-entrance 'sunsaloon' bus body, making it equally suitable for both service duties and pleasure trips, something particularly favoured by small operators at that time. That was followed in July 1930 by a secondhand Reo 'Pullman' 24-seater bus (PY 6490), which had been new to *Redwing Safety Services* of Redcar in Northumberland.

The *Maidonian Bus Service* commenced on Friday 17th January 1930, with a Maidenhead – Littlewick – Knowl Hill – Warren Row – Aston – Remenham – Henley service, with departures from Maidenhead (Bridge) at 8.45am, 10.45am, 11.50am, 1.50pm, 3.15pm, 4.45pm, 6.50pm, 8.15pm and 10.30pm. At that time *Harry* was also offering a 'good 30cwt lorry for general hire and for furniture removal', though the make is not known.

A second bus service was announced in the local press on 4th June 1930, between Maidenhead, Henley and Peppard, though no journey times were stated. Extra journeys between Maidenhead and Henley, by way of Warren Row and Wargrave, were put on for Henley Regatta in mid-June 1930, with buses leaving Henley at 8.15am, 10.20am, 12.45pm, 2.45pm, 4.20pm and 6.40pm, and from Maidenhead at 8.45am, 11.10am, 3.20pm and 5.40pm, whilst 'additional buses would run subject to public demand on Thursday, Friday and Saturday nights', presumably from the Henley end.

This first timetable shows two routes which mostly ran between Maidenhead and Henley (Market Place), but travelling by way of a number of points not then covered by *Thames Valley* or other local operators. In that respect it seems likely that *Harry* had learnt from his private hire customers of a need for such services.

One route set out from Maidenhead (Bridge) by way of King Street (Post Office) – Marlow Road corner – All Saints Avenue – Maidenhead Thicket – Littlewick

(Post Office) – Knowl Hill (P.O.) – Upper Wargrave (Queen Victoria) – Wargrave (Recreation Ground) – Wargrave (Village) – Johnsons Hill – Marsh Mill – Henley (Market Place), though only one journey each way was operated, with the morning departure of 11.40am reaching Henley at 12.30pm. For the rest of its day the bus ran out from Henley to Peppard Common (The Dog) by way of St. Marks Road – Rotherfield Greys (Gillotts Corner) – Rotherfield Greys (Maltsters Arms) – Greys Green – Shepherds Green – Satwell (The Lamb), with 3 or 4 return journeys starting at 12.30pm through to 8.35pm. On most days the 7pm from Peppard ran back through to Maidenhead to arrive at 8.56pm, but on Thursdays, Saturdays and Sundays (for it was indeed a 7-day-a-week operation), the last bus left Peppard at 9.5pm and arrived at Maidenhead Bridge at 10.16pm.

The other service was a more regular link between Maidenhead and Henley, and it also ran all week long, whilst the timetable notes also added that certain journeys at Henley afforded connections with other operator's services to Wallingford and Oxford. That route also started from Maidenhead (Bridge), running via King Street (P.O.) – Marlow Road Corner – All Saints Avenue – Maidenhead Thicket – Littlewick (P.O.) – Knowl Hill – Warren Row – Crazies Hill (The Horns) – Cockpole Green (Old Hatch Gate) – Kentons Corner – Remenham Hill (Five Horseshoes) – Aston (Flower Pot) – Remenham (Church) – Angel Inn and over the River Thames bridge from Berkshire to Oxfordshire and Henley (Market Place).

This service started from Maidenhead at 8.15am, with a last journey from Henley at 6.40pm on Mondays to Fridays, but on Saturdays a 8.40pm departure left Maidenhead returned from Henley at 9.45pm and set down in the centre of Maidenhead at King Street at 10.31pm. The Sunday service ran from Maidenhead at 10am, with four full-length journeys, followed by a short-working out to Warren Row at 9.10pm, which also ran back only to King Street for 10.7pm.

It should also be noted that the 1pm departure on weekdays from Maidenhead ran out to Warren Row only, where the driver took a break until 2.18pm before returning to Maidenhead. Also notable was that the 2pm from Peppard (on the other service) formed a 2.30pm short-working out as far as Remenham Hill, which seems intended primarily for the benefit of schoolchildren.

By August 1930 the Maidenhead booking agent for coach hire and excursions, and indeed the starting point for excursions, had become Mr. Neave Smith the fishing tackle shop adjacent to The Bear Hotel at No.4 High Street, who operated as the agent for *Greyhound Motors* of Bristol and other express connections.

Harry Clinch also included two phone numbers under his own name on the timetable folder, which may indicate that he had some garaging separate from his home address? A parcels service was also provided, with the agents being Mr. Smith in Maidenhead and G. Hinman in the Market Square at Henley.

A notable addition to the excursions programme for September 1930 was a 5-day tour of Devon between 15th and 19th, the advert stating that 'only a few seats were left'.

It is not known for quite how long the irregular service to Henley ran, with its extensions onto Peppard Common, but under the 1930 Road Traffic Act *Harry Clinch* only applied for the stage carriage license in respect of the dedicated all-day Maidenhead – Henley route. That was applied for in May 1931, along with the excursion license for regular Sunday trips from Maidenhead to Bognor Regis and Littlehampton, both of which were duly granted.

Under the provisions of the 1931 Act Construction & Use Regulations many older types of vehicles could no longer be used, and by June 1931 adverts refer to the 'new Maidonian Allweather Coaches', with 14 and 20-seaters on offer, sadly without fuller details known.

The next known timetable of January 1932 shows that the route still ran between Maidenhead (Bridge) and Henley (Market Place) by way of Warren Row and Aston, though the initial outward journey now started from King Street. There were 6 return journeys on Mondays to Fridays, 7 on Saturdays and 5 (afternoon and evening only) in respect of Sundays, all covered by one bus and without the previous short-workings,

The service remained the same at April 1932, though that month he advertised the Chevrolet sun-saloon (RX 5946) for sale in CM, though it actually passed locally to *Fuller & Pomroy (Beta Bus Service)* to continue working from Maidenhead, whilst the following month the *Maidonian* all-weather Chevrolet (RX 4673) passed to a Guildford owner for use as a lorry.

A very popular local event during the 1930's was the Cox Green Flower Show, held each September, which drew large crowds from Maidenhead and, indeed, well beyond. Local operators could be seen running shuttle buses alongside *Thames Valley*, all to a common fare.

From the known information it appears that the bus service continued to be covered by the secondhand Reo (PY 6490), though details of the fleet for that period are certainly incomplete.

In the meantime, *Robert Thackray* had been examining ways of extending the catchment of his Reading – Maidenhead – London express service, particularly after the Traffic Commissioner had refused to license his other established route using the A329 through Wokingham, Bracknell, Ascot and Staines. Apart from putting on a link from Wokingham to the Bath Road at

Upper Wargrave for that same purpose, he obviously saw that residents of the Henley area might be attracted by a cheaper and more frequent link than provided by the branch line railway and its connection to the mainline at Twyford.

With that in mind *the Ledbury Transport Co. Ltd.* (which ran as *Thackray's Way*) put forward a stage carriage license application in April 1932 for a route between Maidenhead (Bear Hotel) and Henley (Market Place), but not over the same road as *Harry Clinch*. Instead, the new service ran along the Bath Road only as far as Maidenhead Thicket, after which it turned northwards to run by way of Burchetts Green crossroads – Temple Golf Club – Hurley (East Arms) – Warren Row turn – Cockpole Green turn – Aston turn – Remenham turn, with an adult single fare of 9d or 1 shilling and 3 pence for a return.

Thackray's ran generally 8 return trips between Henley and Maidenhead, which resulted in a journey time through to London of 2 hours and 7 minutes, and there was a late-night journey which connected with the London-bound coach to reach there at 12.12am. At first the change of vehicles was made at The Bear in the High Street at Maidenhead, one of the famous old coaching inns of the heyday of the horse-drawn stage-coaches along the Bath Road.

Although the route did not follow that of *Maidonian's* service, the end-to-end abstraction of passengers between Henley and Maidenhead soon told on *Harry Clinch's* operation, particularly as *Thackray's* took a more direct routing and used coach-seated Gilford's on the service.

And so it was that *Bob Thackray* and *Harry Clinch* came to discuss the latter selling out, and which resulted in an application in May 1933 to take over the existing service via Warren Row, granted by the Traffic Commissioner on 23rd May. *Thackray's* also noted that each year *Clinch* had provided an enhanced service for the Henley Regatta, which ended with a public fireworks display. In respect of the latter, which had been on the stage carriage license, the new owners also sought approval for the same link, though they would now operate it via the more direct route via Hurley rather than through Wargrave.

An interesting reminiscence of that time recalls that the route via Warren Row apparently carried a restriction to operation by a 14-seater, of which *Thackray's* had no such size vehicles, so one of the earlier Gilfords was down-seated to just 14 seats in order to comply – hardly the point, which of course related to the narrowness of some sections of the road!

At the same time the new operator also dropped the very narrow section serving Aston and Remenham Church, which even in modern days is a stretch for a

16-seater minibus, though the details as printed in Notices & Proceedings do not clearly indicate that.

In October 1933 *Thackray's* asked for a through fare from Henley to London at 3 shillings for a single, and that was approved, which showed the importance of that link, with 'Henley via' being added to the roof-mounted route boards on the coaches above the word Maidenhead. Both the bus services actually terminated at different points in Maidenhead, with the original *Thackray's Way* one having to move away from the congestion of the High Street at the behest of the Borough Council, being relocated around the corner from the railway station in Shoppenhangers Road, whilst the former *Clinch* service still terminated at Maidenhead Bridge.

Arrangements were therefore made for an additional stop on the coach service at the Pond House, a pub on the Bath Road and on the corner with Westborough Road, some three-quarters of a mile from the town centre, where the connections would take place.

Apart from the passengers feeding onto the express services, *Thackray's* also inherited a fair number of school children travelling from the villages to the local secondary schools in Henley and Maidenhead, and special season tickets were made available for their use.

Each of the two bus services were normally approved for operation by two vehicles, though 4 could be used when Henley Regatta was on, and both continued a 7-day-a-week service. No vehicles had passed from *Harry Clinch* with his route, and it was generally the older members of the Gilford fleet that were selected for those duties, but what arrangements existed for their outstationing has not come to light.

From August 1934 the two bus services are shown in the *Thackray's Way* timetable folders as Service No.1 for Maidenhead (Shoppenhangers Road) – Pond House – Thicket Corner – Burchetts Green crossroads – Temple Golf Club – Hurley (East Arms) – Warren Row turn – Remenham Hill (Five Horseshoes) – Remenham turn – Henley (Market Place), whilst Service No.2 referred to the routing from Maidenhead (Bridge) – Bear Hotel – Marlow Road turn – All Saints Avenue – Pond House – Thicket Corner – Littlewick (Post Office) – Warren Row – Crazies Hill (The Horns) – Cockpole Green (Old Hatch Gate) – Kentons Corner – White Hill – Henley (Market Place). Both of these routes would in due course pass with the *Ledbury Transport Co. Ltd.* to *Thames Valley* and became its Routes 16 and 17.

However, despite selling his bus service, *Harry Clinch* was not finished with the local transport scene, continuing with his coaching work until June 1935, when he sold out to *Albert Warwick (Warwick Coaches)*. The latter had originated as a local operator with bus services from his Farnham Common base, but

MAIDENHEAD TO HENLEY.

	Weekdays.								Sundays.				
	AM	AM	PM	PM	PM	PM	S		PM	PM	PM	PM	PM
MAIDENHEAD, Bridge...		1040	1240	2 40	4 40	6 40	8 40	...	1240	2 40	4 40	6 50	8 50
King Street P.O.	8 15	1044	1244	2 44	4 44	6 44	8 44	...	1244	2 44	4 44	6 54	8 54
Marlow Road	8 16	1045	1245	2 45	4 45	6 45	8 45	...	1245	2 45	4 45	6 55	8 55
All Saints Avenue	8 20	1049	1249	2 49	4 49	6 49	8 49	...	1249	2 49	4 49	6 59	8 59
Thicket Corner	8 24	1053	1253	2 53	4 53	6 53	8 53	...	1253	2 53	4 53	7 3	9 3
Littlewick P.O.	8 28	1057	1257	2 57	4 57	6 57	8 57	...	1257	2 57	4 57	7 7	9 7
Knowl Hill	8 32	11 1	1 1	3 1	5 1	7 1	9 1	...	1 1	3 1	5 1	7 11	9 11
Warren Row	8 38	11 6	1 6	3 6	5 6	7 6	9 6	...	1 6	3 6	5 6	7 16	9 16
Craizies Hill, The Horns	8 41	1110	1 10	3 10	5 10	7 10	9 10	...	1 10	3 10	5 10	7 20	9 20
Old Hatch Gate	8 43	1112	1 12	3 12	5 12	7 12	9 12	...	1 12	3 12	5 12	7 22	9 22
Kentons Corner	8 45	1115	1 15	3 15	5 15	7 15	9 15	...	1 15	3 15	5 15	7 25	9 25
Council Houses	8 48	1117	1 17	3 17	5 17	7 17	9 17	...	1 17	3 17	5 17	7 27	9 27
Flower Pot, Aston Ferry	8 54	1122	1 22	3 22	5 22	7 22	9 22	...	1 22	3 22	5 22	7 32	9 32
Remenham Church	8 59	1125	1 25	3 25	5 25	7 25	9 25	...	1 25	3 25	5 25	7 35	9 35
HENLEY, Market Place ...	9 4	1130	1 30	3 30	5 30	7 30	9 30	...	1 30	3 30	5 30	7 40	9 40

	AM	AM	PM	PM	PM	PM	S		PM	PM	PM	PM	PM
HENLEY, Market Place	9 40	1140	1 40	3 40	5 40	7 40	9 40	...	1 40	3 40	5 50	7 50	9 50
Remenham Church	9 45	1145	1 45	3 45	5 45	7 45	9 45	...	1 45	3 45	5 55	7 55	9 55
Flower Pot, Aston Ferry ...	9 50	1150	1 50	3 50	5 50	7 50	9 50	...	1 50	3 50	6 0	8 0	10 0
Council Houses	9 54	1154	1 54	3 54	5 54	7 54	9 54	...	1 54	3 54	6 4	8 4	10 4
Kentons Corner	9 56	1156	1 56	3 56	5 56	7 56	9 56	...	1 56	3 56	6 6	8 6	10 6
Old Hatch Gate	9 58	1158	1 58	3 58	5 58	7 58	9 58	...	1 58	3 58	6 8	8 8	10 8
Craizies Hill, The Horns ...	10 0	12 0	2 0	4 0	6 0	8 0	10 0	...	2 0	4 0	6 10	8 10	1010
Warren Row	10 4	12 4	2 4	4 4	6 4	8 4	10 4	...	2 4	4 4	6 14	8 14	1014
Knowl Hill	10 9	12 9	2 9	4 9	6 9	8 9	10 9	...	2 9	4 9	6 19	8 19	1019
Littlewick P.O.	1013	1213	2 13	4 13	6 13	8 13	1013	...	2 13	4 13	6 23	8 23	1023
Thicket Corner	1017	1217	2 17	4 17	6 17	8 17	1017	...	2 17	4 17	6 27	8 27	1027
All Saints Avenue	1021	1221	2 21	4 21	6 21	8 21	1021	...	2 21	4 21	6 31	8 31	1031
Marlow Road	1025	1225	2 25	4 25	6 25	8 25	1025	...	2 25	4 25	6 35	8 35	1035
King Street P.O.	1026	1226	2 26	4 26	6 26	8 26	1026	...	2 26	4 26	6 36	8 36	1036
MAIDENHEAD, Bridge	1030	1230	2 30	4 30	6 30	8 30	1030	...	2 30	4 30	6 40	8 40	

S Saturdays only.

The Maidonian Bus Service timetable for 1932 as printed on Jade-coloured card. The format of several local operator timetables suggests the same printer, often having some interesting typographical errors – in this case 'Flavor Pot' for Flower Pot (now corrected).

had lost them under the formation of the *London Passenger Transport Board* during 1934, after which he had expanded eastwards through the acquisition of various other firms, adding *Fuller & Pomroy (Beta Coaches)* in March 1935, and then strengthening his hold on the Maidenhead area with *Maidonian Coaches*. Indeed, in a further twist to the local transport history, when *Warwick* acquired *Fuller & Pomroy* he also took over their remaining bus service, which ran from Maidenhead – Hurley (East Arms), operating over the same road between those points as *Thackray's*! At that time the latter was starting to experience some financial difficulties and did not attempt to remove the competition, though in due course in April 1936 it was indeed acquired by *Thames Valley* as its Route 23a, after which *Warwick* concentrated on his coaching facilities with a base at No.31 Marlow Road. More about the activities of both himself and Messrs. *Fuller & Pomroy* will be found under their headings elsewhere in this volume.

As to *Harry Clinch*, he took the Rising Sun pub at Forest Green, south of Holyport, where he remained for a number of years before moving to another over at Winkfield. Latterly he had a smallholding out on the Touchen End to Holyport road, finally passing away in the area at age 84 in 1982.

Albert Victor Cole
Blue Bus Service
Windsor, Berkshire, later Slough, Bucks.

Much of the fuller story of *'Vic' Cole* and his bus operations lies outside the scope of this volume, so after a brief outline, this narrative will concern itself with events affecting the Maidenhead area. The rest of the full history between 1922 and 1969 will appear in a future volume on selected Windsor-based operators.

Having already pioneered a Windsor to Datchet service, and another to Eton Wick, the *Blue Bus Service* was a familiar sight in the town. However, in May 1930 he had given up on the Datchet road, switching the second bus to allow an extension on from Eton Wick to Dorney, with the intention of running through to Maidenhead, but the Council at the latter refused a license.

Under the 1930 Road Traffic Act he was at first refused the license, but was granted it on appeal. Indeed, by then he was not alone on the road between Windsor and Dorney, as the *Marguerite Bus Service* of *Kingham & Watkins*, who are discussed on page 62, so the Traffic Commissioner enforced a co-ordination of timings and fares.

Clearly, that was a drain on his takings, so from November 1931 he increased the frequency through Eton, with a route onwards to Chalvey and Slough, but with 1933 approaching there was a new shadow cast over operations in the Windsor area, with the proposals for the formation of the *London Passenger Transport Board,* which included powers for what amounted to compulsory purchase of existing operations within the designated area. However, when the *Blue Bus* came to be considered, it was decided that Dorney was too far out of the designated area, whilst any attempt to take over the service to Slough via Chalvey would require the co-operation of *Thames Valley,* as part of that lay withing the existing territorial agreement, so in that way, *Blue Bus* became one of the few local survivors.

With the takings on the Eton Wick and Dorney section decreased, *Vic Cole* decided to dispose of his interest on that road to *Kingham,* who was now the sole owner of the *Marguerite* in May 1936, to concentrate on the service through to Slough, which seemed to give *Marguerite* a renewed confidence. But, then in a yet another remarkable twist of events, *Cecil Kingham* decided he wanted to quit the business, so in September 1938 he offered the route back to *Cole*! The latter was only really interested in going as far as Taplow Station, for which there were regular clientele who connected with trains there. But in June 1939 he did apply for the rest of the route through to Maidenhead, but the suspension of normal licensing due to the outbreak of war meant it was not completed. Around the start of the war the Slough service ceased, presumably to save resources, there being alternative services for end-to-end passengers.

Blue Bus Dodge JG 4103 in Thames Street for Eton Wick in early post-war years.

In the meantime, Vic's son *Albert Edward Robert ('Bert') Cole* had served in the Army in Germany from 1926 to 1928, then became a bus driver with *Thames Valley,* not joining the family business until 1933. By July 1948 he running the business, which he did until 1966, when due to ill health, he decided to retire. In the meantime, his son *Ronald* had entered the business in 1955, whilst back in late 1954 the operating base had moved from Windsor to the Bath Road in Slough, even though there was no longer a route to that town.

This former Crosville MS Beadle-bodied Bedford OB bus (HFM 38) had a Perkins diesel engine, and is seen at Maidenhead Coach Station on the Windsor service.

Pressure from Dorney Parish Council led to *Blue Bus* at last seeking the extension onto Maidenhead from August 1957, the bus terminating at the Coach Station in the town. By 1966 *Bert* was not a well man, so it was decided to sell the Windsor to Maidenhead route to *Thames Valley,* so from 4th June 1966 it became its Route 22. However, in order to provide a legacy for *Ronald,* it was arranged in March 1966 for him to take over the service from Maidenhead to Paley Street from *Bray Transport,* who wanted to dispose of it.

In another twist of fate, it therefore became the case that one *Blue Bus Service* took over the service originally operated by another firm of the same title, that having been the Bray operation prior to being reformed in 1948 as *Bray Transport*! *Ronald* ran that route with the trio of buses leftover from the Slough fleet, but it did not really pay, so on 4th October 1969 that was offered to *Thames Valley* as Route 14, duly extended through to Bracknell, as indeed the Bray-based *Blue Bus* had gone in earlier times, whilst the 47-year, 3-generation story of *Blue Bus* of Windsor finally came to its end.

Seen by Mike Penn at the Clock Tower on the forecourt of Maidenhead Station, working the route to Paley Street is Yeates 'Pegasus' - bodied SB5-type Bedford (942 AWR) in May 1968.

George William Collins
The Grenfell
Grenfell Motor Coaches
Maidenhead, Berkshire

George William Collins was born at East Peckham, near Tonbridge in Kent in 1894, the son of a farm baliff. He joined the Army in the early part of the Great War he was stationed at Maidenhead, where he met his future wife Alice Beckett.

His Great War years saw him serve as a Sergeant in the 1st Field Company of the Royal Engineers, taking him to The Dardenelles and Gallipoli, as well as other areas before his de-mobilisation as an invalid in March 1919. He had married Alice in the Summer of 1916, and their son George William James was born in July 1917, followed in due course by sons Jack and Dennis and daughters Enid, Molly and Iris.

On his return to Maidenhead he set up a tobacconist and newspaper shop at No.4 Grenfell Road (see map page 92), was a rather large man of some 25 stone and with indifferent health by old Maidonians. In his youth he had been quite athletic and he remained a keen follower of Maidenhead FC throughout his life.

He was also the local booking agent for *Fuller & Pomroy (The Beta),* but for the 1927 season he decided to add such transport to his existing business. His first intimation of that appeared in the Maidenhead Advertiser on 16th March, stating that he was now offering a coach for hire *(The Grenfell),* details of which are not known. That was followed by another vehicle on 5th May 1927, when a new Reo 'Major', carrying a 20-seater all-weather body, was registered as MO 9980 and had a dark tan livery.

The Reo all-weather coach remained in use for many years, and is seen here with the hood fully fixed up.

Other evidence confirms there were two coaches on offer for that first season, and it is understood that hired drivers were used. Amongst the destinations on offer the first season were the usual coastal resorts and some local tours to take in Virginia Water, Burnham Beeches and The Chilterns. As the year progressed the coaches remained in use with theatre visits to Windsor and also The Alhambra in London, plus the away football matches of Maidenhead FC and the home games of Reading FC, plus some of the 1st Division fixtures held in London. All the excursions departed from Bell Street, just opposite the Station and a short way from his shop, whilst it is known that the coaches were garaged at The Windsor Road Garage, just past the railway bridge, at least in later years.

By January 1930 *Grenfell Motor Coaches* offered 14, 20 and 28-seaters, which implies that the original vehicle was probably the 14-seater, whilst an unknown 28-seater had subsequently been added. The 1927 Reo (MO 9980) remained in use until September 1937, whilst *George Collins* managed to get his Road Service Licenses under the 1930 Road Traffic Act, but unfortunately the details of his fleet over those years is undoubtably incomplete, as at June 1932 there were apparently 14, 20, 26 and 32-seaters available.

Indeed, in an interesting development, *George* announced in the Maidenhead advertiser on 26th November 1930 that 'the *Grenfell Coach Service* is now operating between Maidenhead, Hurley and Henley, via Boyn Hill and Tittle Row – timetables and fares on application'. Such notices continued through to 10th December 1930, but ceased from the following week. It seems that he had intended to create a prior claim to that route before the Act came into effect on 1st January 1931, but given the competition already on that road he probably soon gave up in his attempt.

Another locally lucrative license was to Ascot Races, when an express service was operated at peak times. The business continued throughout the 1930's, and according to a note by the pioneering bus recorder Jimmy LaCroix, a former *City of Oxford* Albion PMA28 of 1930 and with a 31-seater Dodson body (JO 182) was with *Grenfell* following its sale in 1937, whilst he also noted that this coach was later with a showman who over-wintered in Maidenhead.

Car hire had also been added by January 1938, with saloon cars available at 3d per mile, or to meet any trains at the Station from 1 shilling. However, details are rather few though it is understood that in connection with that was The Grenfell Garage in Bell Street.

As already noted, *George Collins* was not a well man, and during 1939 he was ill, culminating in his death at the age of 46 in August 1940. After that his widow continued with the shop and coach and car hire until at least 1946, then with car hire only to 1952. The coach side had continued in a small way through the war years, with it is believed a former *Tappins* of Wallingford 1929 Thornycroft A2Long-type, (RX 3633) was used for a worker's contract. When the decision was taken not to re-equip for a resumption of operations, it was sold to *Carters,* who were happy to further consolidate their holding in the town.

Stanley Jasper Collins
The Alpha
Maidenhead, Berkshire

Whilst the fleetname *Alpha Coaches* was synonymous with *W. F. Cater & Sons* for some 50 years, it was not that firm who originated it in Maidenhead.

Stanley Jasper Collins had been born in 1889 at Reading, but by 1892 the family had relocated to Marlow, where his father Jasper was a shopkeeper in the High Street. However, by 1911, Stanley had moved again to at No.15 Elm Grove in Southsea, where he had set up as a cycle dealer. Although with such a common name, no record of any military service in the Great War, cannot be identified, he nonetheless first appears in Maidenhead at the close of that conflict.

By May 1921 he was at No.7 Marlow Road, when he registered a Crossley WO-type 25hp vehicle as a 14-seater charabanc as BL 8538, painted maroon. It was one of many of that type with military service, many with the RFC/RAF, then being released. Some 10,000 were produced during the war years, and it made for a speedy machine fitted with pneumatic tyres on wire-spoked Rudge-Whtworth wheels, also useful for quick wheel changes if a puncture was encountered, so he was able to state that his *Alpha Charabanc* rode as comfortable as a touring car.

The Crossley BL 8538 is seen about to depart with an all-male party, either a work's outing or from a pub. Note the 2 spare wheels hanging on the rear end!

The first advert in the Maidenhead Advertiser was on 25th May 1921, offering a circular afternoon tour, with one hour's free time at Virginia Water on Thursday 26th at 6 shillings, that day being early-closing for shops in the town. Other operators also used the ploy to bed in a new vehicle on local tours, plus giving passengers an opportunity to try it out. On Sunday 29th his first coastal trip ran to Brighton (65 miles) for 17s 6d. Horse-racing was a sport well followed by Maidonians, so from Tuesday to Friday 2nd to 5th June he ran to Epsom at 15s, and even offered a 4-day ticket for just 50

shillings. The Brighton run had sold out within days, so that was repeated on Sunday 6th June.

The chara was kept at the Amor & East Garage at No.1 Grenfell Road, and excursions started from round the corner at the Clock Tower on Station Forecourt. Trips or private hire bookings could be made at his home, whilst adverts used the slogan 'Enjoy The Country'.

Adverts followed for Wednesday 8th June to Newbury Races for 10s, to Southsea on Sunday 12th for 17s6d, Ascot Races daily from Tuesday to Friday 14-17th, to Windsor Races on 18th June, both at 5s fares, and to Brighton again on Sunday 19th. By then the excursions had moved across the road to The Bell Hotel, due to complaints from the Hackney Carriage drivers at the entrance to the Station, a recurring local issue.

From those public outings many enquiries for private hire followed and, in those days, there was far more of a culture of clubs, church groups and sports and social events, all in need of transport. The small size of the chara lent itself to catering for family hires, sporting teams and dance or darts parties. Indeed, many locals had their first glimpses of the seaside on an *Alpha* trip!

The initial season continued with daily runs to Henley Regatta on Wednesday to Saturday 6-9th July at 5s, to Southsea on Sunday 3rd and Brighton again on Sunday 10th. Later in July further new ground was explored with an outing to the very popular Berkshire Police Sport's Day at Wallingford on Wednesday 20th for 6s 6d, then a circular tour on the afternoon of Thursday 21st to Oxford, out via Reading and Goring, returning via Stokenchurch and Marlow for 7s 6d. Such tours were very popular with the younger shop-workers, as it often gave them a chance to spend time with their boy or girlfriend out of the area. Following that was Brighton once again on Sunday 24th, then to Goodwood Races on Tuesday 26th, with both trips at 17s 6d.

However, it is worth noting that *Bob Probets (The Owner Driver)* was offering seats to Goodwood on his 28-seater for just 13s 6d, demonstrating that the lower capacity could have its disadvantages. On the other hand, the Crossley got there much quicker and more smoothly, so the *Alpha* seaside trips continued to be very popular, with both Brighton and Southsea offered throughout August and September at weekends. The Oxford tour had also been subject to competition, so was reduced to 7s and now featured 2 hours there.

August saw a new afternoon tour on Thursday 25th to Guildford via Farnham and the Hog's Back, with 2 hours at Guildford for 7s. The following Thursday saw Hampton Court offered for the first time at 6s 6d, with a 3-hour stay, and all afternoon tours departed at 2.30pm and returned around 7pm. Bognor Regis was also offered but that necessitated a 7am start!

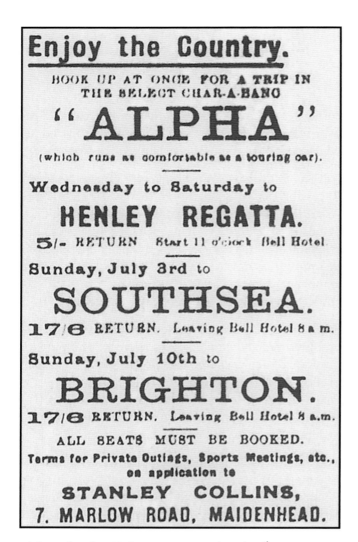

Enjoy the Country.

BOOK UP AT ONCE FOR A TRIP IN THE SELECT CHAR-A-BANC

"ALPHA"

(which runs as comfortable as a touring car).

Wednesday to Saturday to

HENLEY REGATTA.

5/- RETURN   Start 11 o'clock Bell Hotel.

Sunday, July 3rd to

SOUTHSEA.

17/6 RETURN. Leaving Bell Hotel 8 a.m.

Sunday, July 10th to

BRIGHTON.

17/6 RETURN. Leaving Bell Hotel 8 a.m.

ALL SEATS MUST BE BOOKED.

Terms for Private Outings, Sports Meetings, etc., on application to

STANLEY COLLINS,
7. MARLOW ROAD, MAIDENHEAD.

Advert for the Alpha excursions dated 29th June 1921.

One of the dilemmas of the seasonal chara operator was maintaining an income once the weather became unattractive for the outings so far reviewed, though for 1921 he was fortunate in that the Autumn was blessed with fine conditions, so he continued with the circular tours through to October. He then came up with the idea of providing a regular transport to the Windsor Theatre each Tuesday and Saturday, departing at 7pm. With a travel-only fare of 2s 6d. It proved to be a popular attraction, for which he would also book the theatre tickets according to requirements, though in due course he restricted the venture to only Saturdays.

October 1921 also saw trips to Kempton Park Races on Friday and Saturday 7-8th for 10s, plus a 40-mile 3-hour circular tour on Sundays 9th and 16th for 6s. Again, with *Bob Proberts* instead offering a 30-mile trip on 23rd at just 4s 6d, to which Collins retaliated with one on 30th at 30 miles for 5s, but noted he had pneumatic tyres!

However, hibernation did not follow, as on 11-12th November he ran to Hawthorn Hill Steeplechases, 6 miles south of the town, departing at 11.45am, and matching the *Thames Valley* fare of 2s 6d. As Stanley was not then married, he appointed Reg Elston of The Bell Hotel as a Booking Agent in the Town Centre.

The 1922 season commenced on 12th April with an undertaking to 'refund all monies if weather is too bad to set out'! The range of destinations followed that of the initial year, but from 5th July a second 14-seater was available, as well as a 'speedy 1-ton van', which he had probably introduced over the Wintertime, but nothing further is known of it. The second chara was another Crossley of military origins, though this time a 30hp X-type, registered for civilian use as LW 4396.

Another view of the first Crossley BL 8538 on an outing outside the North Star pub in Maidenhead. Note the style of fleetname as used by Collins, most charas of the era only having the name across the rear panel.

A new venture for 1922 was an 11-day extended tour to Blackpool, commencing on 27th August and inclusive of all refreshments en route, but how popular it was is not known. After the usual selection of trips throughout the season, the Windsor theatre outings re-commenced as a Thursday-evening from 12th October, continuing through to Christmastime.

It is not known if Stanley had taken a partner with the second chara, or merely hired a driver, but either way he had shown determination to make a go of it. But, for whatever reasons, over the Winter of 1922/3 he made the decision to give up the business, finding a ready buyer in *W.F. Carter & Sons*, the local taxi and funeral car proprietors, who were considering adding such work. Both the Crossleys passed to them, and probably also the van was the GMC known with them from about that time.

As for *Collins* himself, he is not heard of again in any business capacity locally, so he may have requested employment with the new owner as part of the deal. It is known that in 1939 he was still as PSV Driver, by then at No.26 River Court in Ellington Road at Eton, where he was living with his wife Olive, who he had married in 1930, and he was still at Eton when he passed away in June 1957 at age 68.

Albert Edward Cowley
Lower Road Bus Service
Cookham Rise, Berkshire

The Thames-side village of Cookham is set some 3 miles north of Maidenhead. Whilst many will be familiar with it as a pleasant riverside location, others will also associate it with its favourite son, the artist Stanley Spencer, whose largely devotional paintings were set in the village, often incorporating people he knew. Living in the village, he would have also seen the passing of the *Thames Valley* buses on its High Wycombe – Maidenhead route, for which the Company had to pay an annual fee for crossing the toll bridge to the Buckinghamshire bank.

However, although the *British Automobile Traction Co. Ltd.* reached Cookham in July 1919, and in due course *Thames Valley* continued by extending the service onto Wycombe in July 1920, those buses only reached the eastern edge of the main village. Further to the far end of the High Street, was The Moor, which in turn led to the GWR Railway Station and Cookham Rise, beyond which Cookham Dean made its way up towards the summit of Winter Hill and its fine view over the River Thames towards Marlow. *Thames Valley* had also started a service to Cookham Dean (Church) from Maidenhead in September 1921, as a revised extension of the service to Furze Platt and Pinkneys Green.

Residents also had train connections to Maidenhead from Cookham Station from August 1854, or over the river northwards to Bourne End and onwards to High Wycombe, with a later branch off at Bourne End for Marlow. However, the service was evidently run on a cheap basis and with so many of the roads without lights or footways, those who subsequently provided more convenient bus services found a ready market.

In respect of County Dublin-born *Bert Cowley*, we first encounter him in 1911, when he was 16 years old and living with his parents at No.33 Eton Square in Eton, on the Buckinghamshire bank of the River Thames opposite Windsor, and he was then a motor engineer, a useful trade for a would-be bus operator.

He was the second independent in the area to enter the fray with a bus service in October 1928, at which time he was living at No.8 South View in Cookham Rise. His vehicle of choice was a brand-new Dennis 30cwt registered as RX 3131, and with its 14-seater front-entrance bus body by Willmotts of Shepherds Bush would have cost him around £595. It was perhaps unusual for its size in originally having solid tyres, though that was no doubt a reflection on the state of the local roads, but he did have it converted to pneumatics from January 1930. As with most such small buses it had a front entrance, so the driver issued tickets and stopped the bus for those wishing to alight.

This green and cream-liveried bus ran from Cookham Rise (Lower Road) – Cookham (Station) – Cookham (High Street) – Lower Cookham Road – Ray Mead Road – Maidenhead (Bridge Street) – Maidenhead (Station), and was known as the *Lower Road Bus Service,* which could equally be derived from it using the 'lower' or riverside route into Maidenhead or from its starting point.

The Dennis after entering the Thames Valley fleet as Car 243 (RX 3131), passing the Wellington and white public call box in Maidenhead. The destination box on the front was grafted on by the new owner, as was the case with other buses acquired during that period.

It would not be true to say that the various local small operators were in competition with each other, as by choosing their different points of origin and varied routes, their little buses were well used. When the 1930 Act came into force, each continued much as before. However, after acquiring the *Premier Omnibus Service* of *Reg Robson* in June 1931, *Thames Valley* decided it wished to remove the local competition.

An offer was made to *Bert Cowley,* who was after all just a one-man band of driver-mechanic, in respect of his service and the little Dennis bus. He accepted the offer of £625 towards the end of October 1931, and the bus and route passed to the *'Valley* on 29th of that month. The Dennis became Car No.243 and initially ran in the green paintwork but with *Thames Valley* fleetnames, until it was repainted as red and white by 12th November 1931 and used on the Cookham duties until disposed of in June 1934. At that point its duty was taken over by the similar, but newer, Dennis 30cwt acquired from *Ranger & Simmonds (Reliance Bus Service),* which ran as *TV* Car 261 (GW 540).

William Coxhead & Son
Silver Wings
Maidenhead, Berkshire

William Coxhead was born in 1876 in the Wiltshire village of Aldbourne, the family moving to Lambourn in west Berkshire by 1881, and to Ashmansworth in north Hampshire by 1891, his father being a labourer or carter hired by farmers. No doubt he was one of many young men seeking a better way of life than that.

William married Kate Williams at Maidenhead in 1898, and in 1900 son William Frederick Coxhead was born there, with the family located at No.64 Garden Cottages by 1901, and he was then working as a milkman. By 1911 they had relocated to No.60 St. Marks Road, and *William* senior was by then the foreman at the dairy.

The first vehicle known to have been registered by him was BL 9899, though all that is known is that it was very late 1921 or early 1922. As he is found very soon after that as a coal merchant, it would appear to have been his lorry for that purpose, and by that date they had again moved to 'The Firs' in Penyston Road, and he continued to be found there until at least 1936 as a coal merchant.

In due course his other son, *Arthur Ernest*, who had been born in 1908, was evidently looking for a business venture, perhaps also due to the seasonal nature of the coal trade. Primarily as an avenue for him, father and son formed *William Coxhead & Son*, his elder brother having perished back in 1918 in France aged just 17.

For that venture a new Chevrolet LQ-type was registered RX 6279 on 24th March 1930, and their first newspaper adverts soon followed its arrival. With a 15-seater allweather-type coach body, it bore a blue and grey livery, or perhaps the latter should be regarded as rather more silver, as *Silver Wings* was the name adopted for it.

With the coming of the 1930 Road traffic Act *William Coxhead & Son* gained their share of excursions and tours licenses, though the business was not expanded beyond the single coach, which it seems was driven by *Arthur*. Such work only continued until the 1935 season, and by the following year they were absent in that category in the local directories. However, what became of the Chevrolet is unclear, as it is last heard of as a lorry elsewhere in 1949, so it seems likely it may have served as a coal lorry before leaving the family business. As for William, in 1939 he was still at the same address, now working as a tyre tube vulcaniser, and he duly passed away in 1959 at the age of 82.

Charles Thomas Fuller & Alfred William Pomroy
The Beta, Beta Motor Coaches, Beta Coaches, Beta Bus Services
Maidenhead, Berkshire

Charles Thomas Fuller was born in late 1894 at Merton in Surrey, and by 1911 was living at No.16 Bower Road in Hackney, Middlesex, employed at the family business as a tin whistle maker, the third generation in that trade.

It is most likely that service in the Great War took him to Windsor in Berkshire, where he married Annie

Farrant in 1916, the couple having Frederick, George, Margaret and Leslie in due course.

He joined as a bus driver for the *Thames Valley Traction Co. Ltd.* at its Maidenhead garage in June 1921. His residence at that time was No.74 Boyn Hill, and he continued to drive for them until June 1923 at least, after which he joined the local taxi and jobmaster *William Carter*, who had just added charabanc operation from that season, and he remained with him through to early 1925.

Seen as the centre driver, Charles Fuller and two others prepare for a large outing by Thames Valley's J-type Thornycrofts based at Maidenhead Garage.

Alfred William Pomroy was the son of fish restaurant proprietors Alfred & Fanny Pomroy of No.6 Grenfell Road in Maidenhead, who had come to the town from Devon, evidently having initially reached nearby Bray by 1891, where young Alf was born and his father was then working as a butler by 1901, living at 'Glendale' in Windsor Road.

However, Alf did not enter either that line of work or become involved with the fish'n'chip shop, instead becoming an apprentice motor engineer in Maidenhead when he left school around 1906, being granted his first driving license in 1913, at which point he was living at 'Langholme' at Altwood Bailey on the west of the town, suggesting he was a domestic chauffeur at that date. In July 1915 he joined the army, serving in Egypt with the Army Service Corps before being demobbed as a Sergeant in July 1919, marrying Amelia Rose at nearby Eton upon his return. His mother is also noted as announcing the re-opening of the business in February 1916 after the loss of her husband back in 1913, and she remained in business until at least 1927, passing away in 1939 at age 77.

And so it was that *Charlie Fuller*, with his years of driving experience, and motor mechanic *Alf Pomroy* came together to start their own charabanc business in Maidenhead from the Spring of 1925. Their first advert appeared in the Maidenhead Advertiser during April, noting that they had a pair of 14-seater charabancs, for which they adopted the fleetname *The Beta*. Of course, *Alpha* (as used by *William Carter*) was the originally coined by *Stanley Collins,* though he had sold out to *Carter* in 1923, so *Beta* was chosen not only as the next letter of the Greek alphabet but also for the connotation of being 'better'.

The usual range local excursions and coastal outings to the South Coast were offered throughout the season, but their vehicles remained active with social outings for sports clubs, dance parties etc., and during January 1926 they ran excursions to the pantomime at the Palace Theatre in Reading, all the advertised trips departing from the Bell Hotel opposite the railway station.

At first they used newsagent *George Collins* of No.4 Grenfell Road as their booking agent, but after he took up that line of work in his own right from the Spring of 1927 as *The Grenfell,* they then switched to Mr. J. Francis the tobacconist of No.109 Queen Street instead, at the same time relocating the start place for excursions around the corner to that point from the Bell Hotel (see map page 92).

For garaging they rented space at the Fancourt Garage at No.95a King Street (see map page 27) and opposite the Clock Tower on the Station Approach, the name stemming from the former business of Fancourt & Levington as carriage builders. However, it is evident that only incomplete details are known of the *Beta* fleet, but the identity of the other original chara has remained elusive.

This Reo 'Speedwagon' represented Charles Fuller's half-share of the original pair of charabancs, painted marron and licensed as MO 4927 from 24th March 1925, and it remained in use until the end of 1931.

The excursions of 1927 included Aylesbury, Brighton, Hampton Court, London Zoo, Windsor Theatre and some circular drives taking in Virginia Water or Burnham Beeches during the season, whilst the Winter months saw excursions continuing for Reading Football Club home matches at Elm Park in Reading, along with theatre trips to Windsor. As the coaches had improved in design, so the name *Beta Motor Coaches* came into use, and several longer distance ventures

included extended tours of Cornwall and the Wye Valley.

By September 1928 *Charlie Fuller* had moved to 'Reculvers' in Boyn Valley Road, relocating yet again to 'The Grey Cottage' in Chauntry Road by late 1930, whilst by that date *Alf Pomroy* was at No.6 Portland Road. At some point in 1934 they purchased the confectionary shop at No.107 Queens Road, formerly occupied by Mrs. Edith Hubbard, and later that year the Fuller family moved in over the shop. It should, however, be noted that this was not the No.109 previously mentioned, which remained but was no longer the booking office.

By early 1930 *Beta* could be found travelling even to the away matches of Reading FC and those of Maidenhead United throughout the season. Other over Winter regular outings were to the Chiswick Empire in West London for the theatre and variety shows.

In the meantime, the *Beta* empire was extended by the addition of some local bus services, and it seems that demand for such links came to the attention of the pair through their private hire bookings, many of the points south of Maidenhead not being served by buses.

The exact date of starting is yet to be resolved, but one service provided a new direct link between Binfield and Maidenhead, which by a change of bus at Binfield also opened up links by *Thames Valley* onto Ascot, Bracknell, Wokingham and Reading. The bus started from Maidenhead (Clock Tower) and ran by way of Boyn Hill (The Crown) – Tittle Row (Post Office) – Heywood Park corner – White Waltham (Post Office) – Waltham St. Lawrence (The Bell) – Shurlock Row (Royal Oak) – Allanby Park corner – Binfield (Church) – Binfield Village, terminating on the London Road at Popeswood (Shoulder of Mutton). The through journey took 40 minutes and the full route had a fare of 1 shilling 5 pence for a single or 1s 10d for a return ticket. Only 3 return journeys on weekdays covered the full route, with 2 on a Sunday, but there were also a number of short-workings from Maidenhead to Tittle Row or Waltham St. Lawrence. For some unknown reason there were no press adverts to announce this service, suggesting it was actually the second service to be started and relying on printed timetables?

However, definitely starting on Tuesday 22nd April 1930 was another service from Maidenhead (Clock Tower) which ran on from Tittle Row as Thicket Corner – Maidenhead Thicket (Coach & Horses) – Burchetts Green (The Crown), which took 15 minutes at a single fare of 5d or 7d for a return, with 4 or 5 journeys per day. Both services also offered a post-cinema bus, which left nominally at 10.15pm, though the bus waited by the Rialto Cinema at Chapel Arches until the conclusion of the performance, as was customary at the time. The latter facility was indeed very popular, and the first available timetable of Spring 1931 confirms that 2 buses were required to cover the services.

Another notable addition to the tours for Easter 1930 was a 2-day trip to Ilfracombe in North Devon, whilst more locally there were regular excursions to the Berks & Bucks Staghounds Point-to-Point Races at Sonning, the afternoon outing costing just 2 shillings.

An event that was most certainly a surprise for *Fuller & Pomroy* as well as *Harry Clinch (Maidonian)* took place not long before the passing of the 1930 Road traffic Act, so it might be seen as an attempt by an operator to establish some right to the road? Anyway, on 26th November 1930, *George Collins (Grenfell Coaches)* announced in the Maidenhead Advertiser that his 'Grenfell Coach Service was now in operation between Maidenhead, Hurley and Henley via Boyn Hill and Tittle Row, timetables and fares on application'. Similar notices appeared through to 10th December, but no mentions are found from the edition of 17th December onwards.

In another view of the Reo 'Speedwagon', we again see Charles Fuller with a happy party off for the day. With its pneumatic tyres and 6-cylinder engine, this chara would have been a treat to drive after the ponderous solid-tyred Thornycrofts of his previous employer.

Under the 1930 Road Traffic Act *The Beta Coaches* (as they were now styled) applied to continue both the bus services, which were duly granted Road Service Licenses. Also in April 1931 *Fuller & Pomroy* put forward an application for 34 excursions and tours, but there were a number of objections from other local operators, *Thames Valley* and the inevitable railways, so by the time a successful application was formally granted it had been scaled down to around half of the original, whilst the Traffic Commissioners imposed standard fares between the competitors in the town.

Probably as a result of their thwarted ambitions on the excursions, and following the withdrawal of *Marlow & District* from its Hurley service, *Beta* decided to enhance the service to Burchetts Green by running on to Burchetts Green crossroads – Temple Golf Club – Hurley (East Arms), though there were still shorts out and back to Tittle Row throughout the day.

The intention had also been to extend the service to Binfield onto Wokingham, some 2.5 miles to the west of the Popeswood terminus, and in late 1930 they had made an approach to Wokingham Borough Council, before the 1930 Act took effect, but its inspecting officer for hackney carriages Sargeant Goddard had refused to accept the vehicles. Although the necessary modifications were apparently made and another try made by *Beta* in December 1930, nothing more came of that proposal.

As regards the vehicles used by *Fuller & Pomroy*, it is apparent that only incomplete details are known, and those for which records have survived are shown on page 96.

During early 1933 *Thames Valley* turned its attention to its services in the Hurst and Walthams area, as at the time the various operations were split between its garages at Maidenhead and Reading. In considering how best to recast those services it had also looked at the presence of *Brookhouse Keene (Cody Bus Service)* based at Binfield, who used an indirect routing from Binfield (Jack of Newbury) – Binfield (Church) – Allanby Park corner – Shurlock Row (Royal Oak) – Whistley Green – Hurst – Sandford Mill – Woodley and thence to Reading. In conclusion the Company decided that it needed to acquire both operations, so offers were forthcoming and duly accepted, *Fuller & Pomroy* receiving £850 despite no vehicles changing hands.

From these acquisitions, effective from 1st April 1933, *Thames Valley* altered the *Cody Bus* route only in respect of the starting point moving from Castle Street to Reading Stations, whilst to the east the route now terminated at Shurlock Row (Church). The former *Beta* service was curtailed at Binfield (Standard), the section onwards to Popeswood already being covered by the through service between Windsor and Reading, and the bus now turned west along the Forest Road to finally reach Wokingham but via Warren House. At the same time TV's other operations from Reading to Hurst and Maidenhead to Waltham St. Lawrence, the latter actually pioneered by the former subsidiary *Marlow & District*, were now altered to give a connection between Reading and Maidenhead at Waltham St. Lawrence (The Bell).

Despite the sale of the basic service to Binfield to TV, soon afterwards the early-morning shorts to Tittle Row were successfully added to that of the Hurley timetable. It should also be noted that the terminus of the latter service had been extended further into Hurley to the church with effect from September 1932, which may have also been in order to provide a safer layover point off the main A423 road, with its through traffic and in places poor sight-lines. A timetable for this service is shown on the following page.

Maidenhead (Clock Tower) to Hurley via Boyne Valley Road, Tittle Row, Maidenhead Thicket, Burchetts Green and Temple Golf Club.

		★	★	★	x	★	★	p.m.		p.m.	p.m.	★	p.m.	p.m.	★	★	p.m.	p.m.	p.m.	p.m.	M to F	p.m.	p.m.
Maidenhead, Clock Twr.	dept.	8.30	8.55	10. 0	10.40	10.45	11. 5	12.30		§1.10	1.50	3. 5	3.30	4.10	5. 0	6. 0	6.43	7.30	p m	p m	s8.30	s8.50	9. 0	s9.40	10.15
"Crown," Boyne Hill	,,	8.35	9. 0	10. 5	10.45	10.50	11.10	12 35		§1.15	1.55	3.10	3.35	4.15	5. 5	6. 5	6.48	7.35	s8.35	s8.55	9. 5	s9.45	10.20
Tittle Row, Post Office	,,	8.38	9. 3	10. 8	10.48	10.53	11.13	12.38		§1.18	1.58	3.13	3.38	4.18	5. 8	6. 8	6.51	7.38	s8.38	s8.58	9. 8	s9 48	10.23
Thicket Corner ...	,,	...	9. 5	...	10.50	...	11.15	12.40		...	2. 0	...	4.20	...	...	...	6.53	7.40	...	s9. 0	...	...	10.25
"Coach & Horses"	,,	...	9. 7	...	10.52	...	11.17	12.42		...	2. 2	...	4.22	...	...	...	6 55	7.42	...	s9. 2	...	...	10.27
Burchetts Grn., "Crown"	,,	...	9.10	...	10.55	...	11.20	12.45		...	2. 5	...	4.25	...	...	...	6.58	7.45	...	s9. 5	...	...	10.30
,, ,, + Roads	,,	...	9.11	...	10.56	...	11.21	...		...	2. 6	...	4.26	...	...	...	6.59	...	...	s9. 6	...	...	10.31
Temple Golf Club	,,	...	9.13	...	10.58	...	11.23	...		...	2. 8	...	4.28	...	...	...	7. 1	...	...	s9. 8	...	...	10.33
Hurley, "East Arms" ...	,,	...	9.15	...	11. 0	...	11.25	...		...	2.10	...	4.30	...	...	...	7. 3	...	...	s9.10	...	...	10.35
Church	arr.	...	9.17	...	11. 2	...	11.27	...		...	2.12	...	4.32	...	...	...	7. 5	...	...	s9.12	...	...	10.37

Hurley (route as shown) to Maidenhead Station.

		★	★	★	x	★	★	p.m.		p.m.	p.m.	★	p.m.	p.m.	★	p.m.	p.m.	p.m.	p.m.	M to F	p.m.	p.m.
Hurley, Church ...	dept.	...	9.18	...	11. 3	...	11.28	...		...	2.13	...	4.33	...	...	7. 6	...	...	s9.13	...	10.38
,, "East Arms" ...	,,	...	9.20	...	11. 5	...	11.30	...		...	2.15	...	4.35	...	...	7. 8	...	...	s9.15	...	10.40
Temple Golf Club	,,	...	9.22	...	11. 7	...	11.32	...		...	2.17	...	4.37	...	...	7.10	...	...	s9.17	...	10.42
Burchetts Grn., + Roads	,,	...	9.24	...	11. 9	...	11.34	...		...	2.19	...	4.39	...	...	7.12	...	...	s9.19	...	10.44
,, "Crown"	,,	...	9.25	...	11.10	...	11.35	12.50		...	2.20	...	4.40	...	...	7.13	7.50	...	s9.20	...	10.45
"Coach & Horses"	,,	...	9.28	...	11.13	...	11.38	12.53		...	2.23	...	4.43	...	...	7.16	7.53	...	s9.23	...	10.48
Thicket Corner ...	,,	...	9.30	...	11.15	...	11.40	12.55		...	2.25	...	4.45	...	...	7.18	7.55	...	s9.25	...	10.50
Tittle Row, Post Office...	,,	8.40	9.32	10.10	11.17	10.54	11.42	12.57		§1.40	2.27	3.20	3.55	4.47	5.10	6.25	7.20	7.57	s8.40	s9.27	9.10	s9.50	10.52
Boyne Hill, "The Crown"	,,	8.43	9.35	10.13	11.20	10.57	11.45	1. 0		§1.43	2.30	3.23	3.58	4.50	5.13	6.28	7.23	8. 0	s8.43	s9.30	9.13	s9.53	10.55
Maidenhead, Clock Twr.	arr.	8.48	9.40	10.18	11.25	11. 2	11.50	1. 5		§1.48	2.35	3.28	4. 3	4.55	5.18	6.33	7.28	8. 5	s8.48	s9.35	9.18	s9.58	11. 0

★ Not Sundays.   x Sundays only.   s Sats. & Suns. only.   § Saturdays only.   M to F Mondays to Fridays (incl.) only.

FARES.

Hurley Church
1d.	Hurley ("East Arms")						
2d.	1d.	Temple Golf Club					
2d.	1d.	1d.	Burchetts Green (Cross Roads)				
3d.	2d.	2d.	1d.	Burchetts Green ("Crown")			
5d.	4d.	3d.	3d.	2d.	"Coach & Horses"		
6d.	5d.	4d.	4d.	3d.	2d.	Thicket Corner	
6d.	5d.	4d.	4d.	3d.	2d.	1d.	Tittle Row P.O.
7d.	6d.	5d.	5d.	4d.	3d.	3d.	2d.	Boyne Hill
8d.	7d.	6d.	6d.	5d.	4d.	3d.	3d.	2d.	Maidenhead

RETURN FARES.

Tittle Row Post Office and Maidenhead	...	...	5d.
Burchetts Green and Maidenhead ...	...	...	7d.
Burchetts Green (Cross Roads) and Maidenhead	...	8d.
Temple Golf Club and Maidenhead ...	...	...	10d.
Hurley ("East Arms") ...	...	...	...	10d.
Hurley Church and Maidenhead	...	...	...	1/-

SEASON TICKETS on application.

By the 1934 season the authorised excursions and tours licensed for *Beta Coaches* were as follows:-

Destination	Duration	Notes
Aldershot	Evening	Military Tattoo dates
Ascot	Day	Race Meetings dates
Bognor Regis	Day	1st April – 31st October
Bournemouth	Day	1st April – 31st October
Brighton	Day	1st April – 31st October
Burnham B's	Afternoon	1st April – 31st October
Goodwood	Day	Race Meetings dates
Hayling Island	Day	1st April – 31st October
Hindhead	Afternoon	1st April – 31st October
Leith Hill	Afternoon	1st April – 31st October
Littlehampton	Day	1st April – 31st October
Oxford	Afternoon	1st April – 31st October
Reading	----	Elm Park, Reading
Southampton	Day	1st April – 31st October
Southsea	Day	1st April – 31st October
Wantage	Afternoon	1st April – 31st October
White Horse	Afternoon	1st April – 31st October
Worthing	Day	1st April – 31st October

Note-
A license was also held for express carriages between Maidenhead and Bognor or Littlehampton, which also featured single and period return fares, and day return excursions to those points were not permitted on the Saturdays and Sundays between 1st July and 30th October when that was in operation. The excursions to Reading were for the home matches of Reading Football Club and ran at appropriate times for the kick-off.

Fuller & Pomroy thereafter continued with the Hurley service and their coaching activities through to March 1935, when both were sold to *Albert Warwick,* himself an old established operator originally running buses from his base at Farnham Common, near Slough, until he lost his routes to the *London Passenger Transport Board* in October 1934. He had continued his coaching activities, also adding the Slough – Ascot and Windsor Station – Windsor Racecourse express services of *Walter Freeman* of Windsor.

Under *Warwick* the coaching activities of *Beta* were absorbed, and in June 1935 he added those of *Harry Clinch (Maidonian),* setting up a base at No.31 Marlow Road for his expanded operations, whilst in April 1936 the Hurley service was sold to *Thames Valley,* the latter having already acquired the pair of Henley to Maidenhead bus services with *Thackray's Way* in January of that year.

Charles Fuller had a car hire business after the sale of the bus and coach interests but, unfortunately, he died at the age of 43 in 1938. *Charles* had been living at No.4 Belmont Road in Maidenhead at the time of his death, and his widow Annie could still be found there in 1940 as the local 'Spirella' corset home-fitting consultant.

Alf Pomroy was by 1939 at No.58 Belgrave Road in Slough as a master fishmonger, with he and his wife Amelia also having a fried fish shop taken over from his mother who had died that year, and he passed away locally aged 65 in 1957.

Robert William Gardner
The Harrovian
Harrovian Coaches
Maidenhead, Berkshire

Robert William Gardner was yet another example of a publican-turned-coach operator, his main trade offering good opportunities for gauging public needs, with a ready clientele from the users of his pub at a time when many excursions (Methodist's and Sunday Schools excepted) usually involved a pub stop en route.

He had been born in Bristol in 1887, and by 1901 was a van boy for a laundry. In 1911 we find him living with his parents in the suburb of Westbury-on-Trym at No.233 Southmead Road, when he was working for Bristol Corporation as a labourer. Perhaps noteworthy was that his father was a coachman at that time.

Quite what he did during the Great War is not known, though there were 4 men of that name served in the Army Service Corps. By 1920 he had relocated to Maidenhead as licensee of The Harrow Inn on the Cookham Road in the North Town area.

By late May 1924 he was also offering a 30hp Sunbeam 6-seater landualette for hire for both local work and longer distances, his adverts suggesting that whole families could be taken with their holiday luggage in the car, either to the station or their destination, echoing the practice of some railway companies in providing private buses or 'family saloon' carriages on trains. Other outings were to the very popular British Empire Exhibition at Wembley, and again during 1925, so it would seem that such activities convinced him to try with a larger vehicle.

On 1st June 1926 he entered coach operation with the purchase of MO 7831, a blue-liveried 14-seater chara, which he christened *The Harrovian*. However, the rather interesting fact about that vehicle was that it was one of only four Karrier PSV's sold to operators in the area (other than those of *Marlow & District)*, the others being a pair to *Reading Corporation* and a solitary giant 40-seater chara on a forward-control WL6 chassis to *Bert Butler* of Peppard.

Now, it should be appreciated that the *Marlow & District Motor Services Ltd.* had been set up by the Managing Director of Karrier Motors Reginald Fitzroy Clayton, essentially as a working test-bed for its passenger chassis. One of their bus routes actually terminated at The Harrow Inn, so one can imagine that *Robert Gardner* was doubtless shown over one of their vehicles by its Manager Ernest Jeffries, resulting in an order for a Z-type which was fitted with an all-weather chara-type body by the local (Huddersfield) bodybuilder Joseph Ramsden of Liversedge.

Otherwise, he offered the usual range of coastal trips, long and short excursions to places of interest and special events. He also enjoyed a steady trade with pub teams for darts and cribbage, plus outings to local dances and the theatre throughout the year. Excursions also picked up at Maidenhead Town Hall and The Bell Hotel in King Street.

From June 1927 a Renault saloon car replaced the Sunbeam, though fuller details of each are lacking, and this aspect continued to feature in adverts through to November 1928.

In March 1929 he added a second coach, though not a repeat order for Karriers, as it was a Chevrolet which carried a 14-seater all-weather coach body painted red. It was registered RX 4101, and the fact that this was later re-painted in a two-tone blue livery strongly suggests that it was an off-the-peg purchase from a local dealer's showroom, and with its arrival the term *Harrovian Coaches* came into use.

Under the 1930 Road Traffic Act *Harrovian Coaches* successfully gained Road Service Licenses for a range of excursions and tours starting from The Harrow Inn, and *Robert* continued with the pub until about 1935/6, and as far as can be determined the coaches were kept in the yard of that establishment. By 1933 the Karrier was sold, becoming a lorry, so he continued with just the Chevrolet. From 1936 he moved to No.19 Marlow Road, just to the western side of the town centre, and by then the Chevrolet was garaged at the Cordwallis Works in Cordwallis Road, the former manufactory of the GWK car.

This situation continued through to the close of September 1937, when *Robert Gardner* gave up coach work. Indeed, he is not heard of in the business pages of local directories after that date, though he remained in the town. By 1939 he was working as a porter at Maidenhead Hospital, and died in 1972 at the age of 85.

The Harrovian charabanc was photographed at the coachworks of Joseph Ramsden before the delivery run of some 200 miles south to Maidenhead, probably its longest trip ever. It was almost identical to the Z-type in service with Marlow & District, and it did have the advantage of pneumatic tyres supplied as new.

Gray & Co.
Maidenhead, Berkshire
A Precursor to Pixey

In most cases where local, motor buses became established in the area, the preceding means of passenger transport had been the Country carrier. However, something of an exception existed over the road between Maidenhead and Windsor, which prior to the Great War had been covered by a horse-bus!

William Gray had in fact been born at Windsor in 1852, but after several local moves he was established by 1887 in Maidenhead as *Gray & Co.,* fly and carriage proprietors. At 1891 he was residing to the west of the town centre at No.1 Cambridge Villas, though by 1901 his private address was close by at No.2 Craufurd Rise, whilst throughout the business was based in Marlow Road. By 1895 the Nags Head Refreshment Rooms on the corner of Marlow Road and Grenfell Road was his, listed in 1899 at as hotel, though not of the licensed variety, situated near the Railway Station.

The jobmaster's business continued to offer various forms of horse-drawn transport, but in 1899 the local directory first mentions a horse bus service, which left the Nags Head daily for Windsor at 9.30am and 2.30pm, with return journeys at 12noon and 5.50pm. It also operated on Sundays, with a single return journey out at 2.30pm and back at 6.30pm.

The places served were Holyport, Fifield and Clewer, but the exact route taken is not specified, there being several options, though either way the mileage was around 7.5 miles. The timings show it was intended for pleasure or shopping purposes, and in fact the route would have made a pleasant run on a nice day, the area between the towns being open countryside, whilst it was also an option to travel one way by Salter's Steamers between those towns.

By 1901 William's son Sydney acted as conductor on the service, along with a hired driver, and proof of its popularity was an increase in frequency by 1903, when the outward journeys ran at 9.30am, 2.30pm and 5pm daily, with returns at 12noon, 5.30pm and 8pm, now with the same times for 7 days a week. By then the bus left by the Town Hall in the High Street, opposite the Swan Inn, but the run of local directories available is poor for that period, so although still confirmed at 1911, the service had ceased by 1915. Sydney served in the Army Service Corps in France and Ireland before returning home in 1919 but the service did not return under that family.

However, perhaps residents continued to recall this once lost link, maybe influencing future developments?

Great Western Railway
Road Motors Department
at Maidenhead, Berkshire

For those not familiar with the scope of the operations of the Road Motors of the Great Western Railway, two facts are that they were amongst the pioneers of motor bus services, and duly became one of the largest outfits over a large area of England and Wales.

However, for the purposes of this volume, we will only concern ourselves with the two periods of operation with Maidenhead as a base.

The first era came on 17th June 1911 with services from the Station to Taplow and to Hurley, followed by a route to Holyport from 12th May 1912, for which small Dennis buses were allocated. From 12th May the Taplow to Maidenhead was joined end-on with that to Burnham, but the Maidenhead to Taplow section was discontinued from September 1913. However, with the outbreak of war, resources became an issue, with so many men called up to the Armed forces, so the Hurley service was joined with the Burnham service from 4th May 1914, only to be abandoned from 30th September, 1914, whilst on 11th July the Holyport route had ended.

Despite extensive developments in many other places, it was not until the Spring of 1928 that consideration was given to a return to Maidenhead, the purpose being to provide feeder services to the railhead. The first route of the new regime was out to Littlewick Green and onto to Twyford, which gave a choice of stations for transfer to rail services, as well as for shopping etc., and that started on 2nd April 1928. Other routes were discussed, including acquiring potential competitors, more of which will be found under *Robert Tuck's Yellow Bus* and *West Bros. Blue Bus* concerning the events surrounding the route to Holyport and Jealotts Hill, which the *Road Motors* started on 2nd July 1928.

This Morris-Commercial bus (YW 5365) was one of those covering the 1928 re-introduction of the Road Motors at Maidenhead, seen here on Station Approach. Also note the large rack for parcels on the roof.

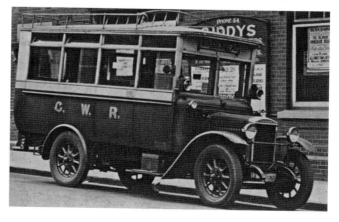

John Henry Harris

Pixey Bus Service
Maidenhead, Berkshire
and later at Fifield, Berkshire

John Henry ('Jimmy') Harris had been born on 7th February 1872 in County Cavan in Ireland, coming to England in 1894, where he worked variously as a waiter, catering manager and chicken-farmer. By 1901 he was at Culvers Corner in Gillingham, Dorset, where he was acting as butler, accompanied by his wife Alice (nee Lawrence), whom he had married at Wayland in Norfolk in September 1900.

In his later years he recalled his early days of driving a horse and cart, which he believed provided a good means of learning safely to drive on the roads, also noting that the higher speeds later attained by motor vehicles was the principle reason for accidents.

By 1905 the couple had moved to Bray in Berkshire, where their son *John William ('Jack')* was born, and *Jimmy's* motor car driving started around 1908. By the Spring of 1909 they were to be found some 3.5 miles further eastwards at No.5 Walter Oakley Cottages in Oakley Green, where he was employed as a valet and chauffeur in charge of a De Dion car.

By the outbreak of the Great War *Jimmy Harris* was not in the age group for general enlistment, but he did volunteer in June 1915. Naturally he was directed to the Grove Park Depot of the Army Service Corps Mechanical Transport at Lea in South London, and his initial posting abroad in 1917 was to France with the 275th MT Company Heavy Artillery, after which he had spells with the 302, 375, 406, 884 and 886 MT Companies, usually driving ammunition trucks to feed the frontline artillery, a particularly hazardous task!

However, he survived to be demobbed in April 1919, and with the war over he obtained a plot of land at Fifield, just about 1.5 miles west of Oakley Green, where he set about (quite literally) building his new family home called Long Lea with his own bare hands, a self-sufficient man, apart from also being a competent motor mechanic.

Given his background and the need to find new employment, he acquired a large Renault car of unknown origins during 1921, which he hired out for private hire and some advertised excursions. His advert in the Maidenhead advertiser for 12th July 1922 states it to have been a 12-seater with hood, side curtains and pneumatic tyres, and it was kept at the Fancourt Garage, No.95a King Street, opposite the Clock Tower and entrance to the Great Western Railway Station.

From 23rd August he started advertising his *Pixey Bus Service,* a name apparently derived from his Irish origins, which ran from Maidenhead (Bear Hotel) to Windsor (Castle), taking in Fifield and Oakley Green, from which it can be deduced he found there was a desire for such a link, and seven return trips were operated on weekdays only at a fare of 9d each way. What was almost certainly the same Renault chassis was now equipped with a 14-seater front-entrance bus body, constructed at the Fancourt & Levington coach-works, which was painted in a pea-green scheme.

The rebodied Renault is seen below with Jimmy at the wheel and his daughter Laura Kathleen, who later emigrated to Canada.

Although the buses of *Thames Valley* took the more direct route between Maidenhead and Windsor, there was competition on an end-to-end basis, and a fares war saw the single trip reduced to 6d by January 1923! In Maidenhead the bus ran from the approved stand by the Chapel Arches, nearby the Bear Hotel and across the road from the *Thames Valley* terminus in Bridge Avenue.

Also, from January 1923 *Jimmy Harris* advertised that the bus could be hired to transport hockey and football teams, theatre or dance parties, with bookings taken at the bus stand or at his Fifield home. At the close of that month he advertised excursions to horse-racing at Kempton, Hurst Park and Sandown, all in Surrey.

At that time the *Thames Valley* buses were suffering from numerous competing operators, so that Company had little time to worry about the *Pixey Bus,* and as the fares war eased *Harris* reverted to a 8d single fare by June 1923. However, he also encountered competition at that time, having to publicly state that 'there was no connection with the brown van over that route'.

The published timetable for June 1923 shows that buses left The Bear Hotel at 10am, 11.30am, 1.45pm, 3pm, 4pm and 7.30pm, returning from Windsor Castle at 10.30am, 12.10pm, 3.45pm, 5pm, 6.40pm and 8pm, so it is evident that *Jimmy* went home for his tea after the 5pm journey from Windsor, returning directly there to take up the 6.40pm departure. By June 1924 there were 9 return journeys, plus a Sunday afternoon service, though the schedule still only required one bus, and now lacked the tea-time break in journeys.

Jack Harris joined his father on the service about 1926, which allowed some expansion. A lucrative local annual event was the Royal Ascot Race Week, held over 4 days in June, and from 1926 the *Pixey Bus* ran twice-daily from Maidenhead direct to the racecourse some 11 miles away, taking both single and return passengers and using Neave Smith as his booking agent at No.4 High Street, opposite the Chapel Arches. For the following season he offered 3 trips at 9.30am, 10.30am and 11.30am outwards at 2s 6d single or 5s pre-booked as a return.

Details of the coming and going of the various vehicles used by are incomplete, being made up of mostly secondhand purchases, plus it is evident that over the years Jimmy collected no less than 9 little Chevies, not all 'runners'at the same time, and son Jack recalled them as 'spread around the long thin yard at Long Lea'.

TM 1258 was a Chevrolet LM-type new in 1927, and is seen by The Guildhall in Windsor.

A list of all known vehicles will be found on page 95, but it is worth noting his one new purchase of RX 1162, a Chevrolet LM-type 14-seater red and white-liveried bus new on 11th November 1927. Also, in view of the number of different origins for his fleet, there does not appear to be a standard livery in use.

At June 1928 the service was still operating from the Maidenhead end at 8d single and 1s 3d return, but from July 1929 it was turned on its head to start from the Windsor end. The reason for this change was the start of another more localised service from Windsor to the new housing areas of Dedworth (The Wolf). After that there were 14 journeys from Windsor to Maidenhead spanning from 8.45am to 10.30pm, after which the bus ran home dead to Fifield. There were also 11 departures from the Castle out to Dedworth, given a 1 to 2-hourly service.

With the advent of the 1930 Act, *Jimmy Harris* was granted the licenses for both of the bus services, along with the 'express carriage' to Ascot Races. However, the passage of that legislation, allied with the shareholdings now taken by the Great Western and Southern Railways in the *Thames Valley* company saw

the latter embarking on an unprecedented spending spree during the 1930's, and particular attention was paid to the Maidenhead area during 1933, with the Board giving its approval to make an offer for the *Pixey* operations on 10th March.

As it was *Jimmy Harris* was now 61 years old and had personally driven on the bus service for some 11 years, so the offer made was too good to resist, with *Thames Valley* paying him £4200 for the goodwill of the two bus services, along with the Ascot 'express' and his collection of 7 little Chevrolets. It should be noted, however, that the written-down value of the latter only amounted to some £130 of that total, whilst the overall payment was much the same as had been made by the *'Valley* for 20 terraced cottages adjacent to the Reading garage in the same period.

And that indeed is what *Jimmy Harris* used his new found capital for, investing in properties in Windsor. Of his buses only RX 1162 (no fleet number allocated) saw any service with the new owners, running from the takeover on 7th April up to 27th of that month, the red and white livery not looking too out of place, after which a Maidenhead-based 1926 Tilling-Stevens B9A was assigned to the Dedworth local service. In respect of the main Windsor to Maidenhead road, *Thames Valley* diverted regular journeys through Fifield village as part of its Route 20. Part of the deal with the *'Valley* was to take his son *Jack Harris* on as a driver at the Maidenhead garage, where he rose to Inspector during the 1960's and retired around 1970.

However, despite his new wealth, *Jimmy* could still be seen in his trademark home-knitted hats and Wellington boots for many more years to come, now as a poultry farmer. Although his wife died around 1942, he remained very active, buying his last car when 93 in 1965, but in 1967 he did finally give up driving. Still known locally as 'Pixey Harris' he finally passed away a fortnight after his 100th birthday in 1972, and Fifield had lost a real character.

Chevrolet LM EF 3469 had a Strachan & Brown body, which had been new to a North-eastern operator in 1927, one of many small operators purchased by the territorial United Automobile Services of Darlington.

Pixey Bus Service BETWEEN Windsor & Maidenhead

LEAVES WINDSOR.

A.M.	8 20	8*50	9*50	10 20	10*50	11 20	11*50
P.M.	12 20	12*50	1 20	1*50	2 20	2*50	3 20
P.M.	3*50	4 20	4*50	5 20	5*50	6 20	6*50
P.M.	7 20	7*50	8 20	8*50	9 20	10 20	10*30

SUNDAYS. First 'Bus from Windsor 11.50 a.m., and then as Week-days

LEAVES MAIDENHEAD.

A.M.	9*0	9 30	10*0	10 30	11*0	11 30	12*0
P.M.	12 30	1*0	1 30	2*0	2 30	3*0	3 30
P.M.	4*0	4 30	5*0	5 30	6*0	6 30	7*0
P.M.	7 30	8*0	8 30	9*0	10*0		

SUNDAYS. First 'Bus from Maidenhead 12.30 p.m., and then as Week-days. * Via Braywood.

Above- An early Pixey timetable after the route was switched to the Windsor end. Below – A fare card as issued around 1931, including local Dedworth trips.

"PIXEY" Bus Service.

FARES

MAIDENHEAD Bear Hotel to		WINDSOR to	
Braywick	2d.	Jutland Lane	2d.
Holyport turn	3d.	" The Wolf "	3d.
Fifield	4d.	" Nag's Head "	4d.
" Nag's Head "	5d.	Fifield turn	5d.
" The Wolf "	6d.	Holyport Cross	6d.
Clewer	7d.	Braywick	7d.
Windsor	8d.	Maidenhead	8d.

H. E. Hewens & Co.
Maidenhead, Berkshire

The motor engineering firm of *H. E. Hewens & Co.* was for many years woven into the fabric of motoring in the Maidenhead area, and through its agencies for Morris and other vehicle makes, often directly involved in the provision of the buses and coaches to the local operators, whilst its extensive premises also formed the base for several operators on a rental basis. In addition, they also became involved in direct charabanc operation for a relatively short period, added to which they were also the first in the town to offer a full-sized purpose-built vehicle of that type.

The founder *Henry Edward Hewens* had been born in Hayes, Middlesex in 1878, and in 1901 he was living still in that area but at Heston, when his occupation is given as Secretary to a Public Company. By 1911 he had relocated his home to just east the of Thames at Taplow, with his motor garage now established a short distance away on the Berkshire bank along in Maidenhead at No.66 Bridge Road, known as Skindles

Garage after the famous hotel and nightspot opposite it on the Buckinghamshire bank.

In July 1915, the very same month that the saxon green buses of the *British Automobile Traction Co. Ltd.* started its original service on the Maidenhead – Reading –Streatley route, it fell to *Hewens* to beat them to it in respect of charabanc work from the town. For that work they registered a new Selden 35hp (BL 039) which was fitted with a grey-liveried 25-seater chara body, and advertised the vehicle for hire, but no public excursions are noted.

The American-built Selden was one of the makes for which the firm held an agency, hence the choice of chassis when much other production has transferred to the war effort, and the vehicle was the only one on offer at Maidenhead throughout the Summers of 1915–1917. It was a 2-ton model with 12ft 6ins wheelbase, fitted with wooden spoked wheels.

There are no clear photos of the Selden chara, but this very similar example operated from Bournemouth. A known photo taken of wounded soldiers convalescing at the Cliveden Hospital was seen by the author many years ago, but copying was not practical, however it is believed it was probably the Selden of Hewen's that was its subject.

Adverts appeared in the local paper through to 15th September 1915, after which it was presumably laid up for the Winter. However, the fuel situation had worsened considerably towards the end of 1917, so the vehicle was disposed of in December 1917, and it went to the General Stores & Munitions Co. Ltd. of London W12 for use as a lorry on war-related service. By then the garage was very busy looking after the vehicles of the Red Cross and those based at the Cliveden Hospital, a few miles away on the Buckinghamshire riverside.

Although *Hewens* did not resume their operation of passenger vehicles after the war, they nonetheless had quite an influence on the supply of vehicles locally, often having several small buses in stock to tempt the operators, whilst it is a fair assumption that the many Morris-built deliveries locally can be attributed to the efforts of their sales staff, and some certainly had bodies built by the firm as well, but unfortunately no records survive. There is also an additional issue in that respect, as Morris also did build its own bodies on such types, so we will probably never know who did what.

Edwin Hodsdon
The Wooburn Belle
Wooburn Green, Buckinghamshire

Edwin Hodsdon had been born at High Wycombe in Buckinghamshire in 1886, and by 1911 he could be found at Aston Rowant in Oxfordshire, where he was employed as a domestic chauffeur. From September 1915 he served in the Army Service Corps in France and was duly demobbed in March 1919, noted as a very competent driver and mechanic, skills he no doubt wished to make use of in civilian life, but away from servitude, in common with many survivors of the war.

Sometime after that he became the licensee of the Old Bell at Wooburn Green, and his entry into passenger travel came when on 15th March 1927 with the arrival of his red-liveried Dennis 30cwt 20-seater coach (PP 7694). The vehicle was christened *The Wooburn Belle*, as a deliberate play on words relating to his other business. The vehicle had pneumatic tyres and was offered for a variety of seaside and more local excursions during the Summer of 1927, driven by Edwin himself. As a local publican he was well-placed to know the local goings on, so various sporting teams were also catered for, along with hires for church and social clubs, the pub serving as the booking office. In June 1927 he disposed of a 2-seater Swift car and a Dodge 15cwt carrier's van, the latter perhaps indicating another transport venture of his at an earlier date, though nothing has come to light through directory entries?

However, it seems that the new business did not work out as he had hoped, so after the first Summer he sold the coach for further service with Maidenhead–based *W. F. Carter & Son,* who ran it under its established name for a year or two before re-painting and re-christening it as *The Maidenhead Belle*, noting it as a 'fully-enclosed luxurious coach with electric lighting'.

A.D. Hooper & Son
The Three Lilies
Maidenhead, Berkshire

We have seen various examples of how charabanc operations were often started in addition to other main trades, but *Albert David Hooper* and his son *Cyril Albert Edward ('Harry') Hooper* are unusual as being boat-builders by trade!

Albert had always lived along the banks of the River Thames, being born at Eton on the Buckinghamshire side in 1868. By 1871 the family had relocated to Friday Street in Henley-on-Thames in Oxfordshire, which led down to the river, and *Albert's* father George (born 1829 in Oxford) and his 16-year old brother George were boat-builders. The family reached Maidenhead by 1881 and were at No.17 Ray Park Cottages, with *Albert* now also in boat-building.

Albert married Ada Simmonds from the riverside village of Cookham in Berkshire in 1892, but by 1893 they were living at No.5 Cobden Crescent in Oxford, all the time continuing to be involved with boat-building. Daughter Mabel Bertha was born in 1893, but by 1901 the family were back in Berkshire at Maidenhead, with son *Cyril* being born in 1903. By the 1911 census we find them living at No.14 Ray Street in Maidenhead, near to the local boatyards. The sheer number of craft of all sizes on the river in those halcyon days of the last years of Queen Victoria's reign, followed by the Edwardian period is exemplified by the well-known painting of 'Boulter's Lock Sunday Afternoon' by Edward John Gregory, so there was lots of work for the local boat-builders.

Throughout the early 1920's there was a general trade depression, whilst many better-off families lost sons who had so much enjoyed those pre-war days on the river, all of which led to a decline in demand for the boat trade. At the same time the post-war development of the motor charabanc, often buoyed by the availability of cheap ex-WD chassis, was well underway. Taking these factors together it can be seen why the *Hoopers* were tempted into charabanc work when the opportunity to build their own arose! They purchased one of the 1000's of WO-type Crossley chassis supplied to the Armed Forces, having come from RAF Ruislip on its release for sale in December 1922 as ME 6153. The 20-25hp chassis was fitted out with a 14-seater charabanc-style body by the *Hoopers,* entering service in March 1923 as *The Three Lilies*, and it continued in use until the end of the 1930 season.

The origins of that name have eluded research so far, being likely to have connection with either the Fleur-de-Lys emblem or possibly a military connection? In due course a large *Three Lilies* sign hung over the High Street office later established by the Bear Hotel in High Street, Maidenhead.

Later, they were able to acquire a secondhand Reo 'Pullman' in chassis only form, its original 1926 body having been scrapped for some reason. It came to them sometime in 1929 from *J.W. Smith (Pride of the Green),* not far away at Wooburn Green in Buckinghamshire, and it was placed in the front garden at their home now situated at 'Iona' in Summerleaze Road, a short way from the riverside. Local eyewitnesses recall that the body took shape rather gradually as time off from the boat-building afforded, and it became something of a local curiosity.

Over that Autumn and Winter the *Hoopers* set about constructing a 31-seater dual-doorway all-weather coach body, the results not being the most stylish seen and incorporating large flowing curves and wings. The coach retained its original registration of PP 6265 when it returned to the road in April 1930.

This rear nearside view is the only one known for the rebodied Reo with its unusual bodywork. Note the enclosed rear wheels, somewhat reminiscent of the covers on paddle-steamers!

Such work was of course still mostly seasonal, so the coach was driven by *Harry Hooper,* whilst both he and his father also continued with the boat-building.

By May 1931 a further secondhand coach had been added in the shape of former *City of Oxford* Daimler CM-type (WL 2187), carrying a Hall Lewis 26-seater dual-entrance coach body new in March 1927. That model had a 16ft wheelbase and 4-cylinder 27hp petrol engine. Also, according to adverts of 1933 a 14-seater coach still featured in the fleet, but its identity has not come to light, though the little fleet is confirmed as 3 then. The capacities of 14, 20 and 26 are quoted, but of course some vehicles may have been altered to meet the new Construction & Use Regulations which, amongst other issues, required offside or rear emergency doors to be fitted to coaches, often resulting in dual-door or multi-door layouts being altered, along with such other features are replacing canvas hoods with a fixed structure, so possibly the Crossley had been re-bodied?

In order to house the coaches a garage was built in Summerleaze Road, where by 1933 the Three Lilies Garage was also undertaking vehicle body repairs, which would seem to confirm that the connection with boats had now ceased completely. The business was known as *A.D. Hooper & Son,* with *Albert* still living at 'Iona'. In due course the garage, and therefore the business address, is given as Blackamoor Lane, though it is believed it didn't actually move, rather more that the extension of Summerleaze Road took on that name as further development occurred there.

Apart from the coaches, there was also a taxi service in operation at least in the 1930's, hence the booking office in the town centre, whilst by 1938 a further booking agent of Mr.Emony, the newsagent at Castle Hill was added and also used as an additional picking up point on excursions. By the Summer of 1932 14 to 32-seaters were on offer. Trips either started from Castle Hill or by The Bear in the High Street, to suit the direction of travel. Some examples from 1932 are-

Day	Date	Excursion	Depart	Fare
Thursday	30th June	Henley Regatta	2.30pm	2s6d
Friday	1st July	Brighton	8.30am	7s6d
Saturday	2nd July	Henley Regatta	1.30pm	2s6d
Sunday	3rd July	Southsea	8.30am	7s6d
Sunday	3rd July	Abingdon/Oxford	1.00pm	5s0d

Apart from the usual mix of excursions and private hire, contract work featured from early on, particularly between Maidenhead and the Slough Trading Estate, some 5 miles to the east. One contract took workers at the 'Aspro' factory, and was generally known by that name, and there are recollections of passengers having to sit under their umbrellas when the ageing canvas-roofed coaches got a soaking!

Albert David Hooper passed away in late 1938, in his 70th year, whilst on the 1939 Register of Population we find *Cyril A.E. Hooper* at 'Gable' in Blackamoor Lane, the next property to 'Iona' as, mentioned earlier. He described himself still as boat-builder and coach proprietor, and he had a lodger who worked at the 'Aspro' factory, so it was quite likely to be the man who drove that contract coach.

A Lancia 'Pentaiota' of 1927 vintage, with unknown coach body and registered FR 7997, was acquired in March 1939 and stayed until June 1945, being used on war-worker's contracts. An unknown make of coach WL 8209, new to *A.R. Collier* of Headington in October 1929 and shown as a 26-seater was recorded in July 1939 by Jimmy LaCroix. The adverts for 1938 give seating capacities as 14, 20, 26 and 32, which suggests the fleet record may still be incomplete or that bodies were altered.

This is the Daimler CF6 referred to on the next page.

A variety of secondhand coaches followed, with a newer model of Daimler, a forward-control CF6-type of July 1930, which carried a 32-seater front-entrance coach body by Duple of Hendon. Registered LJ 1529 it had been new to the famous *Royal Blue* fleet of *Elliott Bros.* of Bournemouth, but arrived at Maidenhead by June 1946 after initially passing with part of the *Royal Blue* operations to *Hants & Dorset*, followed by a spell with *Odiham Motor Services*.

Another 32-seater was also a forward-control Crossley 'Eagle' with a body built by J. Taylor of Barnsley, new in July 1930 to *Retford Coachways* as VO 4394, which had passed to *East Midland*, before coming south by 1946. The newer Daimler and the Crossley replaced the Hooper-bodied Reo (PP 6265) and the CM-type Daimler (WL 2187), with the latter recorded as sold in December 1945.

The Crossley was looking somewhat battered by the time of this photo, but was a rare model indeed.

Despite not having the best of reputations for coaches, it is interesting to note that by 1948 the once-many operators based in Maidenhead had now come down to only the *Three Lilies* and *W.F. Carter & Sons (Alpha Coaches)*.

The first completely new coach arrived in July 1950 in the shape of FRX 598, an AEC 'Regal' 0662-type fitted with a 33-seater front-entrance coach body built by Vincent's of Reading, an example of a pre-war bodybuilder returning to large passenger bodies in the post-war scramble to get more new coaches on the road.

The new 'Regal' replaced the Daimler CF6 (LJ 1529), though the next purchase was actually older than that coach! UU 7131 was a Leyland 'Lion' PLSC3-type and had been delivered new to *United Services Transport* of London SW9 in June 1929, though it is evident that it had been subsequently rebuilt with longer side panels and solid front and rear domes on the Beadle of Dartford dual-doorway 28-seater body, though still with a central canvas section of roof. Also, in common with other examples from that fleet later in use in Jersey, this coach had seen its aged Leyland radiator modified to resemble an AEC-type! It came to

Maidenhead in March 1951 and replaced the Crossley 'Eagle' (VO 4394), which was sold in June of that year.

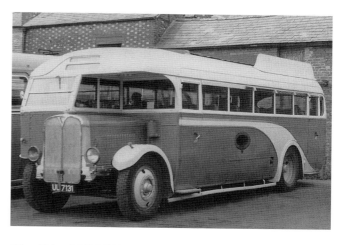

The 'Lion' UU 7131 pretending to be an AEC 'Regal'!

As will be noted from the foregoing, the *Three Lilies* coaches were not the newest types in use locally, and that operator did indeed develop a reputation for not having particularly reliable vehicles! Though they were probably cheap, as at September 1952 they had the contract from the Education Department for pupils from the Furze Platt area travelling to Alwyn Road School in Maidenhead.

The 'Regal' KR 9919 with its 1937 Harrington body.

A further AEC 'Regal' 662-type was acquired in September 1954, being KR 9919 and new in March 1931 to *Autocar* of Maidstone. It had duly passed to *Maidstone & District* through absorption, and in May 1937 it had been re-bodied by Harrington of Hove as a 32-seater front-entrance coach.

The Leyland 'Lion' was still active at June 1953, but was withdrawn by September of that year, followed by the Kent-registered 'Regal' in October 1955, which left only the new-built 'Regal' in service through to its withdrawal in August 1956, though it remained in the area as a non-PSV staff bus with Bingham & Jones, and with that the *Three Lilies* operation finally came to an end, leaving the coaches of the *Carter* family now the sole independents in Maidenhead. As to Cyril, he passed away locally in the Spring of 1965 aged 62.

Edwin Charles Johnson
The Taplow Queen
Taplow, Buckinghamshire

The origins of *Ernest Charles Johnson* were in Marlow, and in fact there is a suspicion that his christian names were originally reversed and he was Charles after his father. Born in 1873, we find him in 1891 as a dairy labourer living near Cookham Railway Station. By 1901 he had married Emily and relocated to No.32 Albert Street in Maidenhead, working as a groom. Then by 1911 he was a carter with a railway contractor, now at No.40 Boyne Hill House in the Boyne Hill area east of Maidenhead. By 1920 he had established The Station Garage at Taplow, and as the name implies it was situated by the Great Western Railway station on the London to Bristol line (some three-quarters of a mile from the village of that name), where he was also its local parcels agent.

His first venture into passenger transport came in April 1927, when he placed a 14-seater allweather-type coach on the road as PP 7877. It was fitted with pneumatic tyres and appears to be a Chevrolet, though the motor tax records have not survived for that mark. Christened *The Taplow Queen*, it must have proven successful, as in July 1927 he added a Chevrolet LM-type, again seating 14 and registered PP 8741. In June 1928 another LM-type 14-seater was placed on the road as KX 666, whilst that month also saw the arrival of a secondhand vehicle. The latter was a Talbot 15hp car of June 1919, which was a popular choice for a small coach, for which new role it was fitted with a 14-seater coach body, retaining the original mark BL 6005. The latter also served as a goods vehicle from January 1932 to April, and it seems an alternative body was available, perhaps in connection with the parcels carrying.

Whether a standard livery was used is uncertain, though records show that KX 666 was in a blue and black livery, though at sometime in 1929 that vehicle was converted to a van still with *Johnson*. The fate of the Chevrolets PP 7877 and PP 8741 are not known.

Little is documented of his excursions, as he did not advertise much in the local press, though he is believed to undertaken the usual mix of coastal and local excursions, private hires and special events. As with all garage-cum-coach operators it was a great advantage having such maintenance facilities, in an age when just getting there and back was by no means a forgone conclusion!

The last vehicle known to have gone to him was another Chevrolet LM-type, UC 1110 and originally described as a 14-seater bus when new in January 1928. It came to Taplow via several other owners in May 1933, leaving again in January 1935, so it is not confirmed to what purpose it was put, though it was a PSV with a further owner. However, it is evident that

Edwin didn't wish to continue such work under the 1930 Act, though he was still running the Taplow Garage at the start of WW2.

Edwin Johnson is seen alongside his Chevrolet LM-type PP 8741, with a party at the coach park by the front at Southsea, always a popular destination for coaches from the 1920's to recent times. A large area had been surfaced with gravel by the Corporation to encourage the charabanc trippers, bringing much money into the resort. Note the removable side-screens, which could be stored in a locker under the body when not in use.

Philip Hugh Keep
B&M Bus Service
Maidenhead, Berkshire

Philip Keep was born at Maidenhead in 1904, the son of Alice Keep who for many years ran a sweetshop at No.50 Bridge Street, opposite the *Thames Valley* bus garage in that town. His father had died when he was about 3 years old, whilst his early employment is not recorded.

In the Spring of 1928 he married Margery Damen, and on 24th March of that year he placed a 14-seater Morris-Commercial 1-tonner bus on the road as RX 1852. It carried a dark brown and beige-liveried body and was supplied by Hewen's Garage, the local Morris agents situated further towards Maidenhead Bridge. In view of the fact that all the subsequent Morris buses, along with a Bedford, came via Hewen's, the varying colour schemes would indicate that these were from showroom stock rather than being built to his specific order. The bus was also kept near to its place of origin, at the motor garage of the Thames Hotel in Ray Lea Road, although his office address was that of his mother's shop.

Although a relative latecomer to the local bus scene, his service did provide direct links not available through the network of *Thames Valley* routes, running as Maidenhead (Grenfell Road for Station) – Bear Hotel – Maidenhead Bridge – Taplow (Dumb Bell) – Drill Hall – One Mile House - Huntercombe – Burnham Station – Cippenham (Everitts Corner) – Burnham Village –

Dropmore (School Corner) – Littleworth Common (for Burnham Beeches) – Beaconsfield (Saracens Head) – Beaconsfield Station.

There are indications from the 1911 census that *Philip* had family connexions with the Burnham/Taplow area which no doubt gave him the knowledge that such a service was desired. It is also interesting to note that his earliest timetable was printed in Beaconsfield and not Maidenhead, despite him being based in that town.

For the service he used the title *B&M Bus Service,* that being derived from the first letters of the two places he linked, and there is no doubt that the service proved worthwhile. On 30th August 1928 he added a second Morris-Commercial 1-tonner, which carried a beige-liveried 14-seater bus body and was registered as RX 2930. It was also kept at the Thames Hotel motor garage, and its arrival saw an additional route added on Saturdays (and Christmas Eve) only.

The extra service ran as Maidenhead (Grenfell Road for Station) – Bear Hotel – Maidenhead Bridge – Taplow (Dumb Bell) – Drill Hall – Taplow Village – Huntswood Lane – Cliveden (Laundry) – Cliveden (The Feathers) – Wooburn Corner – Dropmore (School Corner). With an extra bus free at other times, he also advertised for private hire, which consisted mainly of local hires for sports teams, dance parties etc.

Despite his operating right under the nose of the *Thames Valley Traction Co. Ltd.,* that company made no attempt to compete with these services. Another Morris-Commercial 14-seater bus was added on 13th December 1930, this time painted yellow and as RX 7842. It was followed by a similar bus supplied new by Hewen's in April 1929 to *E.A. Shand (Cream Service)* of Slough, which came back via them to pass to *Philip Keep* from 1st March 1932. It was registered as RX 4003 and is recorded as having a maroon, black and cream livery when it was new.

The timetables for the above services varied very little from the outset, and with the passing of the 1930 Act they continued as before, giving a roughly 2-hourly headway on the Maidenhead – Beaconsfield service and a basic 1-hourly frequency on the Dropmore route, each having a mid-day break for the driver's lunch, the common points along the route also effectively having an enhanced service on Saturdays.

Further fleet changes saw a Bedford WLB with a 20-seater bus body registered as JB 6575 on 4th June 1935 and painted in a red and black livery. As with all other vehicles in use so far, this had a front entrance, all the buses being one-man-operated. The Bedford lasted to the end of the operations, passing for further service with *H.&O. Tibble (Pioneer Bus Service)* of St. Mary Bourne in Hampshire, who used it on their Newbury service through to 1952.

Morris-Commercial RX 4003 has bodywork of a style similar to a number of other local buses on that make of chassis, or on Chevrolet chassis, also known to have been supplied by Hewen's of Maidenhead. It is quite possible that they built at least some of those bodies, or even that they regularly placed such work to the same coachbuilder elsewhere – we shall never know. Note the style of public telephone box then in use behind the rear of the bus, white, not the later iconic red type.

The second Morris (RX 2930) departed with the arrival of the Bedford, whilst the third example (RX 4003) had also gone by 1938. Also joining the fleet was a May 1931 Chevrolet GP 9052, a U-type supplied new to *Keep* and registered by the dealer or bodybuilder, it and the Bedford remained in use until he decided to sell the routes in 1940.

By the Autumn of 1939 Philip and Margery were living at No.76 Bower Way in Slough. The exact details of why he reached that decision are unknown, but it would appear that he found the wartime operating conditions difficult, so he contacted *Thames Valley* regarding the sale of his licenses. The latter were happy to eliminate the local competition, and the services passed to them in April 1940, being re-arranged and extended onto Slough to form Route 22a, which ran as Maidenhead (Bridge Avenue) – Maidenhead Bridge – Taplow (Dumb Bell) – Drill Hall – The Priory – Cliveden (The Feathers) – Dropmore (School Corner) – Burnham Village (The Garibaldi) – Cippenham (Everitts Corner) – Slough Trading Estate (Main Gate) – Salt Hill (Three Tuns) – Slough (The Crown) – Slough Station, so anyone who wanted to go to Beaconsfield would now need to change to *London Transport* buses at Slough. This route was covered by one Maidenhead-based saloon.

No vehicles were involved in the purchase, and the fate of the Bedford is already noted above, whilst the Chevrolet was evidently sold to the Ministry of Supply, with no further users recorded.

At some point after the war Philip and Margery left England, having decided to emigrate to Australia on the assisted Government scheme, and he duly died at Greensborough in Victoria State in 1974.

Cecil Kingham
Robert Harold Watkins
Marguerite Bus Service
Eton Wick, Bucks., later Windsor, Berkshire

The *Marguerite Bus Service* was primarily focussed on linking Eton Wick with Windsor and Maidenhead, but also pioneered a useful link to Taplow.

Of the partners involved in the enterprise, only *Cecil Kingham* had grown up locally, a short way west of Windsor at Oakley Green, where in 1911 we find him aged 8 and living at Kimbers Farm with his mother and her parents. *Robert Watkins*, on the other hand, had been born at Southwark in South London in 1886, marrying Margaret Gough in 1909, by which time he was an engineer living in Walworth. By 1911 he was a motor mechanic and cab proprietor at the Pelham Garage, No.37 Pelham Street in South Kensington. By 1926 he had relocated to Ivy Cottage on Surly Hall Road, by Windsor Racecourse. Given the very closeness of those locations, it must be assumed that the two men became acquainted with each other, though curiously no one in the female lines gives rise to the fleetname *Marguerite*, unless a play on Margaret?

Watkins moved again to Alma Road at Eton Wick, on the opposite side of the River Thames, which became the original base for the bus service, linking that village with Eton and Windsor. In the meantime, *Kingham* had married Violet Ash of Maidenhead in 1924, duly moving nearer to Windsor as Vale Road in Clewer was extended further towards the river at No.113, sometimes referred to as Upper Vale Road. Unfortunately, no timetable issues carried dates, but it must be assumed that the operation commenced with the licensing of a brand-new Chevrolet LQ-type with brown and cream-liveried Willmott 20-seater body, registered as RX 5337 in September 1929. As only *Watkins* is mentioned on the Motor Tax documents, it is possible that *Kingham* did not actually join him until a similar, but secondhand LP-type Chevrolet was purchased in October 1930. New in 1928 it was a 14-seater registered KX 1493.

Unlike *Vic Cole*, whose *Blue Bus Service* only ran between Windsor and Eton Wick, the *Marguerite* went through to Maidenhead from the outset. So, it not only served Dorney, but went via Taplow, evidently to meet the needs of commuters and also schoolchildren, with stops at Taplow Station on the main line and at the Taplow Schools in Rectory Road. The earliest known timetable shows that the Windsor to Maidenhead timings were known as Service A, whereas the Eton Wick and Taplow section was noted as Service B. However, as confirmed from later tables, it was in fact one service. Buses from Windsor on the full route ran as Windsor (Castle) – Eton (High Street) – Eton Wick – Dorney – Taplow Station – Maidenhead (Rialto Cinema), though the latter stop was in fact in the High Street at Chapel Arches. Certain journeys ran onto Taplow Schools, but those did not continue to Maidenhead, but doubled back to Dorney (later Eton Wick). Indeed, the first bus did not reach Maidenhead until 10.38am, showing clearly where the priorities lay.

The original bus (RX 5337) is seen parked by Chapel Arches in Maidenhead High Street, with an ornate sign behind pointing to the Thames Valley bus stands in Bridge Avenue, adjacent to the Rialto Cinema.

TIME TABLE A SERVICE

Windsor and Maidenhead

Sunday to Friday

Windsor to Maidenhead				Maidenhead to Windsor			
Windsor	Eton Wick	Dorney	Maidenh'd	Maidenh'd	Dorney	Eton Wick	Windsor
A.M.	A.M.	A.M.	A.M.	A.M.	A.M.	A.M.	A.M.
10. 8*	10.14	10.22	10.32	10.38*	10.48	10.56	11. 2
11. 8*	11.14	11.22	11.32	11.38*	11.48	11.56	12. 2
P.M.	P.M.	P.M.	P.M.	P.M.	P.M.	P.M.	P.M.
12. 8*	12.14	12.22	12.32	12.38*	12.48	12.56	1. 2
1. 8*	1.14	—	—	—	—	1.56*	2. 2
2. 8	2.14	2.22	2.32	2.38	2.48	2.56	3. 2
3. 8	3.14	3.22	3.32	3.38	3.48	3.56	4. 2
4. 8	4.14	4.22	4.32	4.38	4.48	4.56	5. 2
5. 8	5.14	5.22	5.32	5.38	5.48	5.56	6. 2
6. 8	6.14	6.22	6.32	6.38	6.48	6.56	7. 2
7. 8	7.14	7.22	7.32	7.38	7.48	7.56	8. 2
8. 8	8.14	8.22	8.32	8.38	8.48	8.56	9. 2
9. 8	9.14	9.22	9.32	9.38	9.48	9.56	10. 2
10. 8	10.14	10.22	—	—	10.22	10.30	10.36
10.38†	10.42	10.50	—	—	10.52§	11. 0	11. 6
11. 8§	11.14	11.22	—				

* Sundays excepted.   † Bus waits for Playhouse.
§ Sundays only.

The earliest known timetable, which shows the times for Sundays to Fridays, but only the through journeys, the shorts out to Eton Wick or Dorney not included.

A more intensive service was operated on Saturdays, presumably once the second bus was in use. However, it would soon become apparent that there was not really enough traffic to keep both operators in profit, so it was advertised that buses could be hired for private parties.

TIME TABLE A SERVICE
Windsor and Maidenhead
Saturdays Only

Windsor to Maidenhead				Maidenhead to Windsor			
Wind-sor	Eton Wick	Dorney	Maid-enh'd	Maid-enh'd	Dor-ney	Eton Wick	Wind-sor
A.M.	A.M.	A.M.	A.M.	A.M.	A.M.	A.M.	A.M.
10. 8	10 14	10.22	10.32	10.38	10.48	10.56	11. 2
11. 8	11.14	11.22	11.32	11.38	11.48	11.56	12. 2
P.M.	P.M.	P.M.	P.M.	P.M.	P.M.	P.M.	P.M.
12.8	12.14	12.22	12.32	12.38	12.48	12.56	1. 2
1. 8	1.14	1.22	1.32	1.38	1.48	1.56	2. 2
2. 8	2.14	2.22	2.32	—	—	2.26	2.32
2.38	2.44	2.52	3. 2	2.38	2.48	2.56	3. 2
3. 8	3.14	3.22	3.32	3. 8	3.18	3.26	3.32
3.38	3.44	3.52	4. 2	3.38	3.48	3.56	4. 2
4. 8	4.14	4.22	4.32	4. 8	4.18	4.26	4.32
4.38	4.44	4.52	5. 2	4.38	4.48	4.56	5. 2
5. 8	5.14	5.22	5.32	5. 8	5.18	5.26	5.32
5.38	5.44	5.52	6. 2	5.38	5.48	5.56	6. 2
6. 8	6.14	6.22	6.32	6. 8	6.18	6.26	6.32
6.38	6.44	6.52	7. 2	6.38	6.48	6.56	7. 2
7. 8	7.14	7.22	7.32	7. 8	7.18	7.26	7.32
7.38	7.44	7.52	8. 2	7.38	7.48	7.56	8. 2
8. 8	8.14	8.22	8.32	8. 8	8.18	8.26	8.32
8.38	8.44	8.52	9. 2	8.38	8.48	8.56	9. 2
9. 8	9.14	9.22	9.32	9. 8	9.18	9.26	9.32
9.38	9.44	9.52	10. 2	9.38	9.48	9.56	10. 2
10. 8	10.14	10.22	—	10. 8	10.18	10.26	10.32
10.38†	10.44	10.52	—				
11. 8	11.14	11.22	—				

† Bus waits for Playhouse.

The full timetable for Saturday's busy schedule, which was quite intensive for such a small population in the intermediate places served. Those wishing to travel solely between the two towns could of course use the Thames Valley service on the more direct route.

Indeed, another vehicle was added in 1932, being a secondhand Dennis G-type of January 1929, originally with *North Star* of Stevenage, which was registered UR 2028. At some point in the early to mid-1930's a late 1931 Bedford WLB was also added as UT 9764.

Under the Road Traffic Act 1930 the timetables and fares of the two concerns were co-ordinated at the insistence of the Traffic Commissioner, which seems to further reduced the viability of each, though of course *Vic Cole* also had a Slough to Windsor service as well. Although he extended to Dorney on licensing under the Act, he decided to give up on that route, when he sold his interest to *Kingham* in May 1936, along with a pair of 1931 Chevrolet U-type 14-seaters with bodies by REAL (HX 9680/1). Prior to that, and certainly by October 1935, *Watkins* had dropped out of the service, and by 1939 was living at Runnymeade as Warden of the Monument, to the Magna Carta that is.

Possibly at the ending of the partnership, in March 1935 *Kingham* had purchased a nearly new Ford BB-type as BMX 583, seemingly with private hire in mind, and that was followed by a 1929 Dodge D-type with 20-seat 'sunsaloon' body as VX 533 in January 1936, the latter from Henderson of Brentwood in Essex. However, that was re-sold in November 1937, and in

that same year both the Bedford WLB UT 9764 was sold locally to *A. Moore & Sons (Imperial Bus Service)* of Clewer Hill. These moves seem to indicate that things were not going too well with the bus service or other plans to develop private hire, and no excursion license was ever sought by *Marguerite.*

The Dodge VX 533 had also been used on bus work by its previous owner, but the canvas middle section to the roof also highlighted its suitability for coaching jobs. That American-designed make was by then being built at Kew in Surrey, but PSV sales did not really take off due to the development of the Bedford chassis from its own American counterpart of Chevrolet.

Quite a few timetables for the service are to hand, but none were dated by the operator. Comparison between them, does however show that over the years, attempts were made to meet local requirements, also perhaps to cream off the more lucrative journeys, whilst reducing unremunerative mileage, but nonetheless having two operators plying between Windsor was one too many.

To further confuse the situation, around January 1938, *Kingham* bought a batch of 6 Morris-commercial RP's formerly with *East Kent Road Car Co. Ltd.*, and with operator-built bodies, new in 1932/3. They had been regarded as disappointing by the Kent operator, with all passing to the South London dealer Dawson in October to December 1937. It is not clear if *Kingham* intended to re-equip with these buses, or merely bought them with re-sale in mind. Certainly, none saw use by him, with an advertisement in Commercial Motor soon after he had acquired them in fact. Indeed, only one of them is traced for further use in Ayrshire, those sold to him being JG 2827, 2828, 2829, 2830, 2831 and 2838, all 20-seaters.

However, in May 1938 he sold his operation to *Vic Cole,* who was relieved to lose the competition over the section to Dorney. However, he only wanted to run as far as Taplow, so it was not until 1957, with pressure from the Parish Council, that he finally reached the original terminus of Maidenhead!

Cecil then remained with transport as an articulated lorry driver, still living at Vale Road, finally passing away in 1977.

Ledbury Transport Company Ltd.
Thackray's Way
Reading and London

The town of Maidenhead, situated on the famous Bath Road of the mail-coach era, was well versed in long-distance travel, with its many coaching inns offering refreshment to passengers and fresh horses, in a time before they were eclipsed by the railway.

A second wave of road travel by motor coach had been ushered in with the opening of the Oxford to London service by *South Midland* in 1922, then the *Greyhound Motors* between Bristol and London from 1925, with other operators following as that decade wore on, all of which had a stop at Maidenhead.

In the meantime, the long-established West London cab proprietor and one-time London 'pirate' bus operator *Robert Thackray* had 'retired' to Calcot, just west of Reading. He soon noticed that the express coaches had full loads before reaching Reading, so locals were not able to benefit from those longer-distance services, so he started his own! The fleet of luxurious Duple-bodied Gilford coaches wore a dark red and cream livery and the fleetname *Thackray's Way*, the Reading to London service commencing on 16th September 1929. Such was the success of the venture, that a westwards extension was added from Newbury on 14th October 1929. The service ran via the Bath Road and through Maidenhead and, despite *Thames Valley* having garages both there and in Reading, it did nothing to openly compete with the new operator, merely continuing with its Reading to London limited stop route via Ascot and Staines.

> *The full story of the 90 years of transport history associated with that family was told in the 2001 book 'Thackray's Way – A Family in Road Transport' by the author (£10), still available – see page 92 for website.*

So, within the context of this volume, we will look at the local bus links developed by *Thackray* as feeders to the express service, which he felt was necessary after the 1930 Road Traffic Act brought an end to unfettered expansion. It is said that Robert had some local assistance from *Bob Probets*, which identified that the Pond House, a short way west of Maidenhead, would make a suitable transfer point for passengers to or from a bus link to Henley. And so it was that *Thackray's Way* commenced its service between there and Henley on Monday 5th September 1932, the full route being Henley (Market Place) – Remenham Hill – Hurley – Burchetts Green – Maidenhead Thicket – Pond House, giving a through journey to London of 2 hours and 7 minutes, with tickets issued on the bus or coach service, as conductors were in fact carried on all the coaches.

That road as far as Hurley had already been covered by *Fuller & Pomroy (Beta Bus Service),* though at the time the general state of the economy and effects of the 1930 Act had convinced them to concentrate on the coaching side of that business, so the appearance of the new bus service soon ousted them.

Harry Clinch (Maidonian Bus Service) also found himself in that position, deciding to sell his bus operation and continue with coaching, so on 28th July 1933, his Maidenhead to Henley route was acquired, literally adding another string to *Bob Thackray's* bow. That actually started at Aston (Flower Pot), running west into Henley (Market Place), then turning eastwards up Remenham Hill, before turning off through Kentons Corner – Cockpole Green – Crazies Hill – Warren Row – Knowl Hill – Maidenhead Thicket. With those two routes, hardly any settlement west of the Pond House was not served by the two feeders. However, the section from Aston into Henley was deleted from September 1934, though intending passengers could walk up Ferry Lane to the stop on Remenham Hill.

The Bear Hotel had witnessed coaching along the Bath Road over the centuries, and here it forms the backdrop to Duple-bodied Gilford 166SD-type coach of 1929 UV 7964. Over the bonnet can be seen the shop of Neave Smith, the local booking agent for all coaching services, along with the sale of fishing tackle, plus the then quite scarce public telephone service.

The long and costly saga of competition between the *'Valley* and the *Ledbury Transport Co. Ltd.,* came to a close in late 1935, when the *Tilling Group* provided the funds to buy it out. From 1st January 1936 it was placed under the control of *Thames Valley*, though for various reasons the Company was not wound up until many years later, which resulted in buses running 'on hire' to *Ledbury*, whilst others formed a 'book fleet', but were not only used on its former routes. The pair of Maidenhead to Henley services continued as the *'Valley's* Routes 16 and 17, though they used the Bridge Avenue terminus in Maidenhead, whilst the express coach service became Route B, so the journey from Henley etc. was still possible by changing there.

Marlow & District Motor Services
Marlow, Buckinghamshire

The small brown-and-cream liveried buses of *Marlow & District* were a daily sight in Maidenhead from 1925, and through to 1933, when its identity was lost. From 1929 it operated as a subsidiary of *Thames Valley*, but it to all intents and purposes managed itself.

Its buses not only provided a link between its base at Marlow and Maidenhead, but the services were further developed to provide the local routes from the areas being built up around the town, something that *TV* had been content to leave up to *M&D*.

The bus service brought with it several interesting challenges, as there was not only the elegant but weight-restricted suspension bridge, but the significant assent from the valley floor to the top of Bisham Hill, such factors shaping the fleet even after the *M&D* had long departed the scene.

> However, it is a story already fully explored over 50 pages in the volume *Early Independents of the Henley & Marlow Area*, which can still be obtained – see details of website page 92.

Here we have one of the little Leyland 'Cub' buses as used by Thames Valley in the late 1930's, seen at Quoiting Square in Marlow for the Maidenhead route.

Sidney Robert Probets
The Owner-Driver
Alfred Henry Skeggs
Probets & Skeggs Ltd.,
Maidenhead, Berkshire

Sidney Robert ('Bob') Probets was born at West Wycombe, Buckinghamshire in January 1883, and he duly married Christine Youens at nearby High Wycombe in 1913. By 1901 he had entered the local trade of chair-making, working as a chair-framer, and then lived at No.119 West End Road, in High Wycombe. By 1915 he was the landlord of The Red Lion Hotel at No.34 High Street in Maidenhead, some 10 miles to the south in Berkshire. In 1916 the couple had a son Dennis, but in November of that year Bob joined up with the 30th Lancers, serving until invalid out through sickness in September 1917.

On 25th May 1921 the first advert appeared in the Maidenhead Advertiser for his new additional venture *The Owner-Driver* charabanc. As the name implies, he personally did all the driving in the early days, though the hyphen in the title duly disappeared. At the time he claimed to be the first full-size charabanc operator in the town, and to be fair to him he would probably not of known of the earlier instance of *H. E. Hewens* of such operation, plus of course the Maidenhead garage of the *British Automobile Traction Co. Ltd.* had entered that field from 1919, succeeded by the *Thames Valley* company formed in July 1920 to carry on locally, so it must be assumed he meant it in the sense of independent operations.

Here we see Bob Probets at the wheel of a charabanc which had taken a Work's Outing from Messrs. Cox of Maidenhead all the way to Southend in 1924.

Bookings could be made at the Red Lion, as well as the Saracen's Head Hotel nearby at No.58 High Street, where the vehicle departed from. As both of these premises were old coaching inns dating back a number of centuries, the charabanc was doubtless kept in one of those yards.

Not much is known of the early fleet, but all known photos of 1922-4 show several ex-WD types with full-size chara bodies. The only vehicle known for sure was AEC Y-type (XB 8106), a former WD lorry re-registered in 1920 as a 28-seater chara with *Probets*. Another very likely candidate was an ex-WD Daimler (AN 3830) known from a photo that once hung in The Plough at West End, a pub long ago closed, that appears to be his but the motor tax records for that series have not survived to confirm its ownership.

The initial season started quite modestly on Thursday 26th May with a circular tour to Henley-on-Thames, out via Reading and Caversham and returning through High Wycombe and Cookham, which departed at 3pm and offered an hour in Henley before returning to Maidenhead at 7.30pm for a fare of 6 shillings.

The ex-War Department AEC Y-type charabanc XB 8106 is shown with both Bob Probets and his other driver Mr. Palmer, about to leave The Pond House with a Bun Club outing to Brighton in June 1922. Note that each row of seats is lettered as A to F.

That was followed up on Sunday 29th May by another 3pm departure for Virginia Water, out through Windsor, Runnymeade and Egham, and after a break back via Ascot, Bracknell, Wokingham and Twyford for 7.30pm and a fare of 6 shillings. The third scheduled outing went farther afield to Oxford on Sunday 5th June, departing at 2.30pm, with 2 hours in that city for an 8.45pm return at a fare of 6s 6d.

The Royal Ascot Race Week then followed, with the chara busy on a daily journey on Tuesday-Friday 14th-17th June, leaving the Saracen's Head at 10.30am and calling in at The Bell, opposite the railway station approach in Maidenhead, the return trip being 7s 6d. Thereafter much of the season's trips centred on half-day local excursions on Thursdays, the early-closing day in Maidenhead, with full-day outings on Sundays, and some on Tuesdays and Bank Holidays as well.

The South Coast was first reached by an advertised excursion to Southsea on Sunday 24th July, though there were numerous private hire jobs from local clubs, work's outings and church parties. The other public excursions that season saw the *Owner-Driver* in Aylesbury, Hindhead, Kew Gardens and Watford on half-day tours and to Bournemouth and Southend as coastal trips, plus racing at Goodwood and Newbury.

In late September the 'final excursions' of the 1921 season were advertised as a full-day tour through the New Forest to Bournemouth on Sunday 25th September, a half-day excursion to Oxford on Thursday 29th September and finally an afternoon tour via Hampton Court and Bushey Park on Sunday 2nd October.

However, the Autumn of that year proved a very fine one for weather, and *Bob Probets* followed the lead of *Stanley Collins* and his *Alpha* charabanc in offering some circular trips taking in the Thames valley and Chiltern countryside. Whereas *Collins* had offered a 40-mile circular at 6s, *Probets* countered that with a 30-miler at 4s 6d, resulting in *Collins* revising his to 30-miles, though at 5s fare, a mini fares war in fact!

The final advertised chara outing by the *Owner-Driver* occurred on Sunday 30th October, after which it would have been expected that the vehicle would be laid up for the Winter months. However, as driver on these various outings, *Bob Probets* was well aware that many locally were not entirely happy with the bus service provision to their localities.

At some point in late September he started to run a bus service between Maidenhead to Burchetts Green and Pinkneys Green, *Thames Valley* having recently reduced its services to those points. The latter did soon respond with additional journeys, forcing *Probets* to abandon that operation with effect from Wednesday 5th October, but no further details are known of the days and times of operation.

Above - *The Owner Driver advert for excursions from The Maidenhead Advertiser of 25ᵗʰ May 1921.* *Below -* *Adverts such as this of 16ᵗʰ November 1921 charted the rise and fall of Bob Probets efforts to provide local bus services, which were both a genuine attempt to open up links he was made aware of during his charabanc operations, whilst also keeping a vehicle employed.*

Above – *Announcement of 31ˢᵗ November 1921, and* *below –* *the swansong advert for 14ᵗʰ December 1921.*

Despite the above sequence of events, he was not dissuaded from such ventures, and from Friday 21ˢᵗ October 1921 he put on two Fridays and Saturdays-only services, one southwards some 3.5 miles from Maidenhead to Holyport and Touchen End (Hinds Head), and the other westwards to Tittle Row, Camley Corner and Burchetts Green, about the same distance. The latter caused a clash with the established services of the *Valley,* so he altered his Burchetts Green route to run via Pond House and Littlewick Green (Post Office). Journeys left for there from Maidenhead (Bear Hotel) at 9.45am, 11.55am and 3.10pm, returning from Burchetts Green at 10.10am, 12.25pm and 3.35pm. The same vehicle also covered the Touchen End route leaving Maidenhead at 10.35am, 1.15pm and 4.30pm and returning at 11am, 1.40pm and 4.55pm, the timetable also noting that the latter route ran via Bray village.

On 2nd November 1921 *Probets* felt obliged to publicly announce that the 2d fares being used against him by *Thames Valley* were unrealistic and that he would continue running, so evidently the larger firm had opted for a fares war, a common short-term tactic.

However, he still used his local knowledge to his advantage, adding a late-night bus from Maidenhead to the Touchen End service on Fridays and Saturdays from 11th November 1921. Of course, in those days many people had work on Saturday, so from 16th of that month the late journey only ran on Saturdays, and it left at 10.15pm to cater for cinema patrons and other entertainments in the town. By 16th November the service to Touchen End had been enhanced, now departing from Maidenhead on Fridays at 10.35am, 1.15pm, 4pm and 5.30pm, whilst Saturday travellers had a choice of 10.35am, 1pm, 1.50pm, 4pm, 5.30pm and 10.15pm. All was not however well on the route to Burchetts Green, and a fortnight later it is noted in the newspaper adverts as 'temporarily suspended'!

Another new operation, also dove-tailing in with the Friday and Saturday Touchen End service started on Friday 2nd December 1921 from Maidenhead a distance of some 6 miles to White Waltham via Boyn Hill and Cox Green, with the 3 journeys from White Waltham at 10am, 12.30pm and 3.30pm. It should be noted that *Bob Probets* had a good following for his chara work from those areas, which no doubt inspired the decision to run out there.

For the period leading up to Christmas extra days were operated on both the White Waltham and Touchen End routes on Wednesday/Thursday 21st/22nd December, but after that no further adverts appear for the *Owner-Driver* bus services. Indeed, the withdrawl of the Touchen End operation seems to have been the catalyst for local haulage contractor *Bob Tuck* to enter passenger transport with his *Yellow Bus Service,* and full details will be found elsewhere regarding that venture.

The *Owner Driver* (now without a hyphen in adverts) re-appeared with conventional charabanc work from late March 1922, including an advance advert for a 5-day tour of Devon, which was successful and repeated several times more that season and in subsequent years. Otherwise, it was the usual mix of coastal full-day excursions and more local half-day outings, with bookings now made at either the Red Lion or the Bon Marche Library. Several points of interest were that he offered a full refund should the weather be so bad that the trip did not set out, whilst he also noted that it was the only charabanc in the town to carry two drivers for

passenger safety, and this may well have been when the aforementioned Mr. Palmer joined him.

Bob at the wheel of a chara again, this time leaving The Foresters pub at Cox Green with the Football Club on an outing to the seaside.

It could have been surmised that *Bob Probets* was no longer interest in bus operations, but on 4th October 1922 he informed the public that both the Touchen End and White Waltham services would run again on Fridays and Saturdays! He even added another route some 3 miles east-wards out to Lent Rise and Burnham on those same days, though no times are known. However, no further adverts followed, so no conclusions can be made on how long any of these ran for, and no subsequent bus operations were attempted by him. It should be noted that the '*Valley* was by then employing its 14-seater Ford 'chasers' against other operators along the Slough – Maidenhead – Reading road, whilst it was also now in a stronger position in respect of vehicles and crews than it had been in 1921.

Charabanc work continued throughout the 1923 season, with adverts referring to 'closed in coaches with electric lighting', plus motor car hire, whilst the 1924 British Empire Exhibition at Wembley saw the *Owner Driver* charas very busy, leading to further expansion that season. Additional destinations for that year were to the Aldershot Military Tattoo on the evenings of 18th-20th June at 6s 6d, Regents Park Zoo (and its new aquarium) at 5s 6d, Brighton for 10s 6d and the numerous Wembley runs at 5s per head. In respect of the latter, the same rate applied to private parties to that destination, amongst which was that of the employees of the Maidenhead branch of McIlroy's Stores, who were even paid for the day as a treat by their generous employer.

Although *Probets* had carried on at the Red Lion during this time, at some point in 1924 he relinquished the license and moved to Nos.52/54 High Street, and by May 1925 he was also the local booking agent for the Bristol – London coach express service of *Greyhound Motors*. From the Winter of 1925 he also offered motor repairs and driving instruction, followed in January

1926 by a weekly motor haulage service to Manchester, Bristol, Liverpool and Birmingham, as well as towns en route.

The AEC chara XB 8106 is shown again with owner and Driver Palmer, this time outside Hyman Lewis, the fancy goods shop at No.11 High Street, with Achille Searle, cleaners and dyers, flanking Alexander's Café.

It should be noted that Maidenhead Borough Council was not particularly active in respect of hackney carriage regulations, other than the matters of stands for cabs and some routing restrictions for buses, so unfortunately there are no meaningful records of the vehicles used locally from that source. However, at that time the excursions departed from The Saracen's Head at No.58 High Street (see map page 92).

In July 1925 his adverts refer to 'air-cushioned tyres' on the coaches, whilst in June 1927 seating capacities of 14, 20 and 28 are quoted, whilst in May 1929 all were 'all-weather, centre-gangway' types. In respect of the cars available, an advert of June 1927 refers to 6-seater Daimlers with open and closed bodywork. An addition for the 1927 season was a 5-day tour to Devon, which was offered annually for some years.

From late 1927 an interesting, indeed perhaps intriguing, connection commenced with the mighty *Southdown Motor Services,* with the acquisition of an unknown make of 20-seater charabanc, new in 1920 to *Southsea Tourist,* which came to Maidenhead in December. That was followed in November 1928 by a pair of Harrington chara bodies of 18 and 27 seats new in 1922 to *Southdown.* All of these sales were in respect of bodies only, so it is not known to what chassis they were fitted by *Probets.* However, it is known that an AEC chassis was given the '5-series' treatment, a scheme for updating WD-era Y-types by extending the chassis and fitting a 5-series AEC A109 -type engine in place of the original Tylor unit. This is known from an advert in Commercial Motor for 8th October 1929, when it was offered for sale. It may well have been the original XB 8106 which was so rebuilt and rebodied?

The last mention of the *Owner Driver* operational name came in February 1930, when the address changed from the High Street (above Boots the chemist in the town) to 'Southdown House' on the Bath Road at Taplow, just to the east of Maidenhead. The next month saw the formation of a new company under the title of *Probets & Skeggs Ltd.,* motor coach operators of No.12a High Street and No.4 Norfolk Road, Maidenhead, the latter address also being *Bob Probets* residence. There were a few instances where the old title appeared alongside adverts up to July 1930.

The new partner in the business was *Alfred Henry Skeggs,* born in 1886 in Hertford, but by 1911 he was living in Maidenhead at No.25 Cordwallis Street, employed as a general labourer, and no other details of how the partnership came into being have come to light, though he arrived due his marriage in 1909.

With the coming of the 1930 Road Traffic Act in January 1931 *Probets & Skeggs Ltd.* applied for Road Service Licenses for Excursions & Tours to start from The Bear Hotel, no doubt in continuation of practice at that time. These consisted of full-day outings to Bognor, Bournemouth, Brighton, Cheddar, Eastbourne, Epsom, Goodwood, Hastings, Kempton Park, London Zoo, Margate, Southampton, Southend, Southsea, Weymouth and Worthing. Half-day tours ran to Ascot, Aylesbury, Hampton Court, Hindhead, Kew Gardens, Leith Hill, Oxford, Reading, Thame Show, Tring Show and Virginia Water, whilst evening excursions took in the Aldershot Military Tattoo and Burnham Beeches, the daily maximum of coaches in use being 4.

At the same time, they also applied for a selection of E&T's starting from Victoria Street in High Wycombe, these covering full-day runs to Bognor, Bournemouth, Brighton, Cheddar, Eastbourne, Hastings, London Zoo and Southsea, all of which would pick up at Maidenhead en route. The application in respect of Maidenhead was fully granted, but that from High Wycombe was the subject of objections from other local operators, as well as *Thames Valley,* and it was therefore refused.

Adverts for April 1931 state 14 and 20-seaters had been added to the fleet, but fuller details are lacking, though the bodies may have been derived from those purchased from *Southdown* and modernised? Yet another *Southdown* connection came in July 1932, when that company agreed to sell another vehicle to *Probets & Skeggs* on hire-purchase terms. The vehicle in question (BK 2881) had started out as a Dennis 3-tonner when new in 1919 to *Southsea Tourist,* but in 1926/7 the chassis had been lengthened, fitted with a new Dennis E-type engine, and then re-bodied in 1927 with a new Harrington 30-seater coach body, and it was in that updated form when it came to Maidenhead.

Dennis BK 2881 had been extensively rebuilt when with Southdown MS, so by the time it came to Probets & Skeggs it resembled a Dennis F-type, and is seen here when still with Southdown. Unfortunately, a number of the fleet are not represented by any photographs, so fuller details regarding their appearance are not known.

By June 1932 on offer were Rolls Royce cars which could be hired for longer journeys at 6d per mile.

For quite how long *Probets & Skeggs* remained as coach operators has yet to be resolved, but in 1936 *Bob Probets* only is noted in local directories, under car hire and 14 to 32-seater first-class coaches at No.12A High Street, Maidenhead, whilst *Alfred Skeggs* had returned to his old area at Tongwell by 1939, where he was a public works contractor. The last mention of coaches came in March 1938, thereafter entries for *Probets* continue through to at least 1948 but for car hire only. However, in the next available directory of 1955 we find *Probets Car Services* (with proprietor H. Humphrey) at No.12a High Street, *Bob Probets* having passed away in 1950, whilst *Alf Skeggs* had preceded him back in 1940.

Cyril Apsley Ranger
Alfred Simmonds
The Orange Bus, Reliance Bus Co.
Maidenhead and Slough

Both *Ranger* and *Simmonds* commenced their separate operations during 1922, there being no connection between them at that time, so we will firstly examine the activities of each of them in their early days.

Alf Simmonds was of unknown origins, but by May 1920 we find him at 'The Pines' in Upton, near Slough

in Buckinghamshire. On the 29th of that month he placed BH 9063 on the road, though it was at that point just a Ford Model T car with seats for 6 passengers. In putting it on the road between Slough and Windsor, he was joining another dozen or so other independents racing their small buses between those towns. It soon became obvious he needed to increase his capacity, so the Ford was fitted with a chassis extension kit, after which it was re-bodied as a 14-seater bus, returning to service in July in a red livery with *Reliance Bus Co.* painted along its sides.

In November 1922 that was joined by another 14-seater on modified Ford T-type chassis, often referred to as the 'Ton-bus' or TT-type as BH 9638, when the route was extended to run as Maidenhead-Slough-Windsor. There is apparently some reason to connect him to a garage business in Maidenhead, but the author had not discovered that in the local directories. Indeed, it is known that his buses were kept in a shed built next to his home and the kerbside had a ramp to aid their passage. A third Ford T, with Baico chassis extension, was purchased secondhand as BY 1492 with a 14-seater body, which he licensed from September 1923.

However, the unbridled competition of so many small concerns racing buses between Windsor and Slough had led to numerous complaints from other road users, as well as the *Thames Valley Traction Co. Ltd.*, so both

Councils decided that in future only operators showing a responsible attitude would have licenses renewed, and also that the only way new entrants could do so was by purchasing an existing license. Alf realised that the road was over-bussed, so he sold his Windsor-licensed BH 9063 to aspiring operator *George Thomas*, and he left the Windsor road from 8th February 1924. After that he concentrated on the Maidenhead to Slough service.

Ford BY 1492 seen with Alf outside his Upton home.

Cyril Apsley Ranger was not born locally, though his mother had hailed from Maidenhead, and he was born at Worplesdon in Surrey in 1897, one of 9 children, his father being a retired miller and corn merchant. By 1913 he was at 'Merlewood' on Woodbridge Road in Guildford, having started as an engineering apprentice with Dickensen & Burne in that town.

With the outbreak of the Great Way he joined up in April 1914, then in July 1915 went as part of the Mediterranean Expeditionary Force, being injured and returned to England via the Egyptian port Alexandria, then duly sent to France as the war reached its close. After that he was demobbed in February 1919 and married Lois Pym at Maidenhead.

By then residing at No.17 York Road, Maidenhead he commenced a service between there and Reading, despite that road being covered since the precursor of *Thames Valley* with its green-painted *British* buses from the Summer of 1915. He had obtained a license for his unknown make of 14-seater bus registered MO 572 on 21st November 1922 from Reading BC, and used the title *Orange Bus*, from which we must conclude that was its livery. However, he soon found a pair of Ford T-type 14-seaters on his heals, as *TV* unleashed its 'chasers' against him! As MO 773/4 they bore no fleetname and being all-over red, they were dubbed locally as the 'scarlet runners', the tactic being to race ahead with one bus and use the other to block him in, all highly illegal, but widespread practice by even the most 'respectable' of outfits!

Reading BC had not helped matters either, as it had directed various operators to use the Market Place to avoid what it perceived as traffic congestion, which in hindsight was obviously to protect its trams!

The '*Valley* also employed its other usual tactic of reducing fares, something it could bear in the short term, but harmful for the competition, and these tactics led to *Ranger* placing an appeal in the Maidenhead Advertiser of 28th December 1922, which read as –

'An Appeal – The bus fares on the Maidenhead to Reading route have been subject to drastic reductions, and I would beg all my friends who have loyally assisted me in the past to ALWAYS travel by the Orange Local Bus, and so enable me (an ex-soldier) to gain an honest livelihood. You will gather that I am unfortunately unable to stand in St. Mary's Butts, but if you will grant my application for patronage, you will be doing good work, and I shall be most grateful'.

Believe me, yours obediently, C. A. Ranger

Timetable –

Leave Maidenhead	*10.10*	*1.55*	*4.35*	*7.15*
Arrive Reading Market Place	*11.10*	*2.55*	*5.35*	*8.15*
Leave Reading Market Place	*11.55*	*3.15*	*5.55*	*8.35*
Arrive Maidenhead	*12.55*	*4.15*	*6.55*	*9.35*

At that time the '*Valley* was using Thornycroft J-type double-deckers on solid tyres on that road, so the small bus took 10 minutes less over the full route. Indeed, the General Manager of *Thames Valley*, T. Graham Homer, had noted the competition in his quarterly reports as abstracting passengers from its service.

Quite how and when Cyril and Alf first met up is not recorded, but each had encountered similar difficulties in the course of trying to make their living in those times of high unemployment in a land less-than-fit for heroes. In due course *Simmonds* also applied to Reading BC for a license, or perhaps that actually marked the start of a partnership? Anyway, he was granted a license on 19th June 1923, placing his Ford 14-seater BH 9638 on that road.

Whatever the exact catalyst, full co-operation soon followed, when the pair each purchased an identical Berliet 20-seater bus in March 1924, both painted red and white. The French-built model VMBL was at the time enjoying sales with a number of independents, being quite nippy buses, though time would show them as problematical. One was registered MO 2850 for *Alf Simmonds,* replacing BH 9638 on the license, whilst MO 2851 was *Cyril Ranger's* replacement for MO 572. A third example, which was licensed by *Ranger*, but on behalf of the *Reliance Bus Company*, followed as MO 3558 in July 1924. It was noted on the Motor Tax papers for MO 2850 that it was kept at the Amor & East Garage at No.1 Grenfell Road in Maidenhead.

An illustration of a Berliet bus from a magazine advert.

Although the *'Valley* had employed the little chasers, by then they had been sent to the Ascot area to deal with more pressing competition, leading to relative calm on the Maidenhead to Reading road. However, in the GM's quarterly report for September 1925, it was noted that all 3 of the *Reliance* Berliets were off the road, and it was added that the older buses then in use were not attracting much patronage!

Indeed, *Reliance* offered to sell the business to TV in November 1925, but the amount requested was considered too high, as it included 6 buses that the *'Valley* did not want. If true, then clearly, not all the fleet at that point are recorded. But it is known that the Ford BH 9638 was still in use over on the Maidenhead to Slough route, and in February 1925 a Thornycroft J-type with 26-seater bus body was added as MO 4695.

It then became clear to the partners that they would never be tolerated on the route to Reading, and by the end of the year the service had ceased, all efforts then being directed to enhancing the Maidenhead to Slough operations.

All the Berliets had gone during 1927, but did find further users nonetheless. One of their replacements, which came at an unrecorded date was a 20-seater on a Reo 'Speedwagon' chassis new in March 1925 as SP 9878 to *Smith* of Kirkcaldy, believed licensed from October 1926 to *Reliance.*

However, the territorial *Thames Valley* was soon noting the increased competition on the Maidenhead to Slough road, upon which it had recently sent a batch of 'new' 32-seaters on Thornycroft J-type chassis rebuilt to forward control. But, on the other hand, *Simmonds* had used his local knowledge to provide the journeys that the locals wanted, so quite a pattern had developed to serve various points, including going through the Slough Trading Estate at peak times, the full route with that deviation being as Maidenhead (Station) – High Street (Bear Hotel) – Maidenhead Bridge – Taplow (Dumb Bell) – Lent Rise – Burnham Village – Everitts Corner – Slough TE (Dover Road, Hamilton Road and Main Gate) – Salt Hill (Three Tuns) – Slough (Crown Hotel) – Slough (Station). The last trip waited by The

Bear for the conclusion of the performance at the Rialto Cinema just across the road, and the timetable confirms all buses were now garaged in Slough. However, Cyril remained in Maidenhead, though by 1931 he was at 'Hebron' in Forlease Road.

The only instance of advertising for an excursion was in 1927, when buses were run to the evening Military Tattoo at Aldershot on 14th-18th June, the fare being 5 shillings, bookable at the shop 'Doris' by The Bear.

At June 1928 the *'Valley's* GM was complaining to the Maidenhead and Slough Councils about licensing other operators between those towns, and to up the pressure it had now put Tilling-Stevens saloons on that service to enhance the frequency.

Another vehicle known to have been used became available from June 1929, a Dennis G-type 14-seater with Strachan & Brown body, new to *Orange Coaches* of Chatham in August 1927 as KO 4530. During June 1929 the by then rather dated ex-WD Thornycroft J-type MO 4695 was sold to become a lorry for a Reading owner, a common fate for such basic types.

The firm experienced a bad accident about 6pm on Friday 3rd January 1930, when there was a collision between one of its buses and a locomotive operating for the Slough Estates. That area was linked to the main rail line, and within its confines the engines moved wagons around, often running alongside roads or across them in places. It was a very wet day, so Charlie Allen, the driver of the 14-seater had reduced visibility, which led to him not seeing the loco as it crossed in front of him, the two modes of transport coming together in a smash which wrote the bus off. The incident occurred along Buckingham Avenue, resulting in 5 passengers needing to be taken to King Edward VII Hospital in Windsor, whilst others were dealt with for cuts and bruises by the local ambulance.

In response to that sudden loss of a bus, a new 14-seater Dennis 30cwt was purchased from the dealer and coachbuilder Willmott, who registered it as GW 540.

The Dennis GW 540 at Slough soon after it arrived.

Quite a boost came for the fleet in April 1931, when that same firm supplied a trio of Dodge 14-seaters as RX 8373-5, all in a red and white livery.

The improvement in rolling stock was needed, because *Thames Valley* had now switched its newer 35-seater Tilling-Stevens B9A saloons on the Maidenhead to Slough route, with the frequency now at 10 minutes.

That Company, now buoyed up by the financial interest of the Great Western Railway, was busy buying out the competition in an era of 'cheque-book diplomacy'. It met with *Ranger & Simmonds* in the Spring of 1933, which resulted in the independent ceasing after 27th May 1933. The deal included the 4 buses bought new in 1930/1, but all were initially placed in store at the Maidenhead Garage. The Dodge buses were soon put in an advert, but the little Dennis did enter the *TV* fleet a year later as Car 261 (GW 540), when it took the place of the similar bus formerly owned by *A.E. Cowley* as Car 243 (RX 3131) on the Cookham services, a duty it stayed on until disposal in July 1936. TV paid £4700 for the buses and the goodwill, and they soon found buyers for the three Dodges to offset some of that.

RX 8373 went to E.G. Beech of Liskeard, and it is likely that the GWR Station displayed may have been on the original blind with Reliance? It is also believed to still be in the red and cream livery as when new.

RX 8375 went nearer to home, passing to W. Bulman & Sons of Hook Heath, near Woking in Surrey for their local bus service, and is seen outside their garage still looking quite presentable.

Although there are reasons to believe that additional buses were owned, that is the Slough BC Hackney Carriage records show changes and capacities which do not tally with the known fleet, several vehicles noted in London Buses Volume 3 were certainly not as listed, so I must make mention of that just for the record –

RX 4101 is shown as a Dodge, but was in fact a chara owned by *Robert Gardner (Harrovian Coaches)* of North Town in Maidenhead, a Chevrolet new to him and retained until he ceased operation in September 1937.

The other was quoted as RX 4530, almost certainly an error for KO 4530, as the Berkshire mark was used for a motorcycle.

What became of *Alf Simmonds* is not known, but *Cyril Ranger* was still a PSV driver in 1939, living on the Bath Road in Slough, though when he died in 1973, he was living in the Eastbourne area of East Sussex.

Reginald James Robson
Premier Motor Omnibus Co.
Cookham, Berkshire
Including Henry William Jordan
and John William Jordan
Station Garage, Cookham

The origins of passenger transport ventures from the railway station at Cookham go back to *Henry William Jordan*, who had been born in the village in 1857. He actually spent much of his working life as a bricklayer employed on the construction of developing areas in West and South London, but had returned to the area by 1891, when he was living in Dean Road, and by 1899 had established himself as a fruiterer and fly proprietor. By 1901 that had become a carman and fly proprietor, whilst his son *John William ('Bill') Jordan* was driving the fly for him, having been born in Chelsea in 1882. By 1911 Henry had expanded as jobmaster, coal merchant and farmer, now at Dean Farm, aided on the farm by sons Ernest (19) and Henry (15). He carried on the jobmaster's business alongside farming through to at least 1920, and in 1911 36-year old Ernest Corke was his coachman.

However, *Bill Jordan* broke away from working for his father by 1911 to become the local *Great Western Railway* agent, handling incoming and outgoing parcels, being paid by the railway to deliver items locally, and at that time he was living at 'Thornhills' in Cookham Rise. What he used as transport initially is not recorded, but by 1920 he had established the Station Garage, adjacent to the railway station.

On 30th January 1920 he registered a Ford Model T 1-tonner with a wagonette type body as BL 6849, in a red and cream livery and as a public conveyance. Whilst he did not run a timetabled bus service as such, he did meet the trains for parcels, and the provision of seating, along with previous fly experience, strongly indicates that passengers were a regular trade, also with the station serving a rather spread out local area. When the vehicle came to be re-declared under the 1920 Road Traffic Act in January 1921 it was shown to now have two alternative bodies, one being a lead-coloured goods body and the other a van-chara with 13 seats, which was probably the wagonette body now with a canvas top. It continued in use by him, though latterly as goods only, until June 1927 when he sold it to his father for use on the farm.

In the meantime, *Bill Jordan* started motor taxi work to cater for passengers to and from the station, using a couple of quite antique Daimler cars, usually driven by Arthur Wilsden and his son 'Bunny' of Station Road. Although the cars were old, they were both reliable and comfortable. Wilsden could be found on the 1911 census in Station Road, working as a carter.

Reg Robson had been born at Paddington in 1894, seeing service in the Royal Engineers in France from November 1915. He evidently returned to the London area from 1918 through to 1922, as in that year he married Constance Flavell at Wandsworth, at which time Reg was an electrical engineer residing at No.64 Sisters Avenue, Clapham.

Exactly when the *Robsons* came to Cookham is not known, but evidently *Reg Robson* soon realised there was a need for a faster and cheaper link to Maidenhead, and on 4th August 1925 he placed a Morris T-type 1-ton 14-seater front-entrance bus (MO 6078) on that route, bearing a red livery and entitled *The Premier Omnibus*. Although no original timetable has been discovered, the route is believed to been Cookham (Station) – Cookham (Tarry Stone) – Lower Cookham Road –Ray Mead Road (Boulters Lock) – Maidenhead (Bear Hotel) – Maidenhead (Station). In due course this was extended to start from Cookham Dean (Chequers Inn) and travel to Cookham (Station) via Cookham Rise. In 1925 the couple were living at No.4 Romanlea in Cookham.

The little Morris bus was evidently found to be a good purchase, having been supplied by the local main agents Hewen's Garages of Maidenhead, and on 11th June 1927 a larger 30-cwt Z-type example was registered as RX 215. That carried a 20-seater front-entrance bus body painted as red and white, and by then they had relocated to 'Woodbank' in Cookham Rise, no doubt having a relevance to the extending of the route to take in that area as well.

A further expansion occurred in April 1928, when *Reg* took over the Station Garage business from *Bill Jordan* who, according to a local resident of the time 'had let his drinking habits get the better of him'. The Daimler taxis were also inherited, along with their old drivers, whilst the buses were also now kept there. After that

Bill could still be found as coal merchant, collecting his supplies from the railway yard.

With the advent of the second bus, advertised as the 'new Premier de-luxe motor bus with 20 comfortable bucket seats and giant pneumatic tyres', some excursions were now offered. The first of these were to the ever-popular Ascot Races during June, for which the bus left Cookham (Station) at 10.30am, calling en route at Maidenhead (Bear Hotel) at 10.45 for a return fare of 5 shillings.

A number of other excursions followed between June and October 1927, both locally and further afield, whilst the buses were available for hire when not otherwise engaged. With a nice enclosed body it was of course practical to continue beyond the close of the coaching season, and from September to November 1927 he advertised a Thursday-evenings departure at 6pm into Reading for the theatres and cinemas, with a return run at the conclusion of performances, which of course could also be enjoyed by the driver.

Not that *Reg Robson* was now the sole driver, as George Gore joined him with the arrival of the second bus. The Daimler taxis continued in the care of the Wilsdens, whilst Charlie Fenner was the mechanic for the small fleet at the Station Garage., also driving when required.

For 1928 the Ascot Races excursions were again repeated, though no other advertised excursions were undertaken, and this probably marks an increase in the frequency of the bus operations, though private hire was certainly still continuing at other times.

In April 1929 the body was removed from Morris 1-tonner MO 6078 and re-mounted on a new Dennis 30-cwt chassis and registered as GU 7544.

The Dennis is shown after painting by Thames Valley as Car 239, now fitted with a destination box on the front dome. Note the distinctive diamond-shaped rear panel on the sides, a feature so far not identified on any other bodies of that period, so its builder remains a mystery, not even being recorded by Thames Valley.

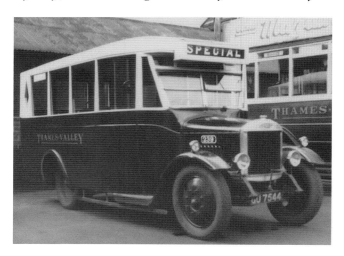

Following the involvement of *Great Western Railway* shares in the *Thames Valley Traction Co. Ltd.*, the latter was actively encouraged to remove competition, which after the 1930 Road Traffic Act meant purchasing the Road Service Licenses held by operators. Indeed, when the *'Valley* contacted *Robson* in April 1931 such license applications were still with the Traffic Commissioner, though it is reasonable to assume his service would continue. *Thames Valley* offered him £850 for the service and the Dennis bus, writing to the Traffic Commissioner on 10th April to take over the license as applied for in March by *Reg Robson*.

At some point prior to 1931 the Maidenhead terminus had been altered from the Station Approach to nearby in Grenfell Road, though this occurred with a number of such services as the forecourt became crowded by taxis and cars, though timetables often did not have their description of Station altered as such.

Robson had evidently disposed of the Morris 30-cwt bus (RX 215) prior to 1931, as the application sought an hourly service on weekdays between 8.55am until 8.55pm, followed by a 10pm journey from Cookham, whilst on Sundays buses ran hourly from 2.55pm to 8.55pm and then again at 10pm, handled by one bus.

The application went through, including the change of applicant, and *Thames Valley* took over the service from Monday 8th June 1931, and as the services in the area were being further reviewed it did not initially get a route number, but was duly known as the 23a to complement the existing Maidenhead – Furze Platt – Pinkneys Green – Cookham Dean Route 23. The first the public knew of the takeover were the handbills in the bus windows, a typical *'Valley* ploy of that time!

The little Dennis was one of a number of non-standard types coming into the *'Valley's* fleet around that time, and was repainted and became Car 239, seeing some limited use on its old duties until it was decided to use secondhand Thornycroft Car 238 (RX 188) instead from October 1931. In view of its rather short career, and that there was an order for 3 new coaches in hand at Brush Coachworks it was decided to re-issue the number to the first of those Leyland 'Tiger' TS4's, so the second Car 239 (RX 9307) took that identity from November 1931.

As *Thames Valley* wanted to work the route from the Maidenhead Garage, the timings were modified with a bus leaving there at 7.55am to form the 8.25am into town, after which buses left hourly from Cookham at 25 past through to 9.25pm, followed by a last bus back to Maidenhead at 10.30pm, the whole day covered by the one bus. The acquisition of *Reg Robson's* service by the *'Valley*, soon to be followed by that of *Bert Cowley*, would leave only the *Dean Bus Service* of *Chastell & Gray* of the three Cookham-based independents left as the local competition.

After a short time the Dennis was re-sold quite locally to B.G. Howse (Brown Bus) of Englefield Green, passing with that operator into London Transport in March 1934, and is shown withdrawn after use at the Amersham Garage.

In 1932-4 directories Reg is still shown as motor car proprietor at The Station Garage, but absent from 1936, when that business was with another. According to local informants the Robsons then took a pub in Cookham, though no further details have been found, but in 1939 they were indeed in that trade at Nos.13-15 Lower Boston Road in Ealing. However, they had evidently returned to the area, as in 1948 Connie is recorded at 'Murrayfield' in Cookham Rise, whilst when *Reg Robson* passed away in March 1956 he was still in the local area, Connie dying that same year.

Map showing the positions of the various settlements in the Cookham area, the River Thames and roads.

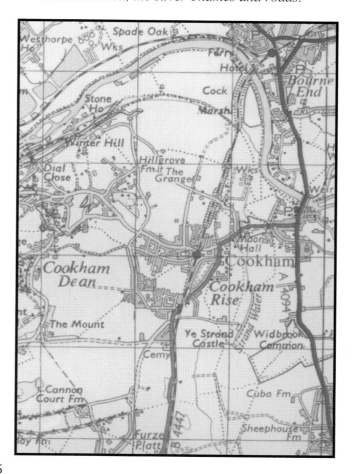

Joseph William Smith,
later Leonard Smith
Pride Of The Green
Wooburn Green, Buckinghamshire

'Bill' Smith had been born in December 1875 at Harrow in Middlesex, duly marrying Florence Wingmore there in 1897. At that point he was a plumber, but for the 1911 census, we find him at No.50 High Street in Wealdstone, near Harrow, where he is trading as an oil and colourman, a mixer of printing inks and paints. Their son *Leonard* was born in 1913 at Hendon, but otherwise their whereabouts are unknown until after the Great War.

We first encounter him with a transport venture, and also at Wooburn Green in Buckinghamshire in 1921, that being situated some 5 miles south of High Wycombe and 6 miles north-east of Maidenhead, the village centred around a large green as suggested by its name. In February 1921 he placed a Commer on the road as BH 1825, which had alternative bodies for use as a lorry or bus, which confirms his involvement with both forms of transport from the outset. That was added to in July 1924 with a 1916-built Straker-Squire CO-type (LP 8653) with 32-seater bus body, which stayed until November 1925. Another Straker-Squire was owned at unknown dates, a 20-seater (NH 686) but its origins are not known. Exactly what the passenger vehicles were used for is unknown, but presumably on private hire and some excursions.

Bill's address on acquiring NH 686 was Vernon House, but the site for the yard was certainly opposite the green, so he had adopted the fleetname *Pride Of The Green* by the time the first new purpose-built coach arrived in May 1926 as PP 6265, a Reo 'Pullman' with 26-seater all-weather body. That was joined in May 1927 by a Chevrolet LM-type (PP 8301), with 14-seater body, then by a similar LQ-type 14-seater in March 1929 as KX 2273.

Unfortunately, the Reo suffered from a major accident, possibly a fire, during 1929, and it was sold as a rolling chassis to *Hooper & Son* of Maidenhead, so its fate can be found detailed on page 57. As a replacement a 1928 Reo 'Pullman' 20-seater was acquired as YW 3479. In April 1930 another Chevrolet, this time a U-type with 14-seater body was purchased new as KX 4772, the little Chevies having been further refined over the years.

No evidence whatsoever has come to light of adverts for excursions, or indeed the haulage side, both of which continued in parallel throughout the 1920's and '30's. The coach fleet as described above remained quite stable until May 1932 when a Duple-bodied 20-seater Bedford WLB-type (the successor to the Chevrolet chassis) came as KX 8621, then a new 'big' Dennis 'Lancet' was added in March 1937 as AJB 520, the latter having a 32-seater coach body by Dennis.

Few WLB-type Bedfords lasted beyond the early '50's, and most were with seasonal coastal operators, so the continued use of KX 8621 was notable. As shown here at the yard, it was evidently kept in as-new condition.

Withdrawals of the earlier types are mostly unrecorded, and some may have transferred to the haulage fleet for a time. The Bedford WLB was remarkable in staying until 1958, but the Dennis was requisitioned in 1940 and did not return. In respect of a livery, the original Reo and the Bedford wore a grey livery, which is taken to be the usual scheme applied to the fleet.

At some point Bill's wife Florence had passed away, and during the Summer of 1939 he re-married to Ann Matlida Pratt, whose family had long been established with a shop on the Green. As it happens, her mother Matilda had come from Hackney in East London, but certainly had local connections as she had married Charles Pratt in Hackney on Christmas Day 1865, the only day he could get off from his bakery at Wooburn Green, which went back to at least 1861. Ann was born in 1884, and duly helped her mother in the shop, her father having passed away in 1912.

So, that union led to even more diverse business in the village, all giving a good ear to the ground for trade on the coaches and for the lorries. The yard had developed over the years to house a shed for the coaches, plus at the end of it was another one for the local Volunteer Fire Brigade, with *Bill* himself holding the post of Chief Fire Officer for some years, the early post-war contingent consisting of two Bedfords, one towing a pump and the other an ex-WD QL-type as a tanker, very familiar mechanically to a man brought up on the Chevrolets and Bedford chassis of his own operations.

Exactly what the coaches did during the war years is not detailed, but along with the lorries, there would have been plenty of war-related contracts to occupy them. After the war one lorry was used to collect wood-pulp from the railway station for transport to Glory Mill at Glory Mill Lane, whilst a daily passenger contract took workers to the Screw Machine Products factory in Holtspur Lane, probably of wartime origins in itself.

Gurney Nutting-bodied Bedford LEL 882 is seen with lettering for Screw Machine Products, but is on hire from Smith to Jeffways & Pilot of High Wycombe.

Such was the relevance of such work, the Company was allocated one of the famous utility-bodied OWB-type Bedfords as HBH 331 in 1943, originally fitted with wooden seating for 32 as new. Post-war the excursions and private hire continued, alongside the haulage work, the known vehicles being detailed on page 112. *Bill* passed away in 1952 aged 77, but son *Leonard* continued through to 1972, when *Pride Of The Green* finally ceased.

Robert Tuck
Yellow Bus Service
('The Mustard Pot')
Touchen End, Berkshire

Robert Henry Tuck was born in 1873 at Woodstock in Oxfordshire, having a quite varied life before entering our story. By 1878 the family had relocated to the Crown Hotel in the Market Place at Faringdon, then in Berkshire, where his father was an ostler. The horse theme was probably continued with his enlistment in the cavalry of the 2nd Dragoon Guards, when at 1891 he is found at Northgate Barracks in Canterbury, Kent. We next find him still in that capacity, but as a prisoner detained at Judd Street Police Station in St. Pancras, London, still a single man in 1901. Quite what followed that event is not known, but in 1911 he was at Ottawa in C′ ∩da, having married and emigrated there in 1905! It   known is he duly returned to England, ′   ·ice in the Great War. That possibly is   to the area, through the Canadian   Cliveden?

Bob Tuck is first encountered with transport on 28th August 1922, when a 2-year old Ford Model T 20hp goods vehicle (BL 7814) passed into his ownership. By then his home was at No.6 Council Houses, one of a row of six of such semi-detached properties on the main road at Touchen End, near Holyport, undertaking haulage and removals work.

However, back on Friday 21st October 1921, another local operator had reached Holyport and Touchen End with a bus service. That was *Sidney Robert ('Bob') Probets*, proprietor of the *Owner Driver* charabanc, and he offered 3 journeys from Maidenhead, running on Fridays and Saturdays only from The Bear Hotel to the Hinds Head by the Paley Street turn at Touchen End. In response to popular demand a 10pm bus from Maidenhead was added from 9th November, though from 16th it became Saturdays only and re-timed at 10.15pm to better suit cinema patrons. At the same time the general frequency of the service was altered to give 4 journeys on Fridays and 6 on Saturdays.

Probets continued to advertise the above service, along with other local operations, until October 1922, after which time he concentrated his efforts on chara work, along with car hire and driving tuition. It would seem that the local residents much missed this service, causing *Bob Tuck* to consider filling the void.

Although the above Ford was duly re-bodied as a bus, or provided with an alternative body, it was the purchase of a similar vehicle new on 30th August 1923 which appears to mark the start of the bus operations. This 14-seater bus (MO 2060) was painted yellow in line with the official title of the venture as the *Yellow Bus Service*, also earning it the nickname *The Mustard Pot,* after the well-known brand of Colman's Mustard!

The service ran from Maidenhead (Grenfell Road) to Bracknell High Street (Hinds Head), travelling by way of Braywick Road – Holyport (Green) – Paley Street Turn – Touchen End – Hawthorn Hill – Jealotts Hill – Warfield (Battle Bridge) – Warfield Road (Wick Hill). For this venture *Bob Tuck* was joined by drivers Emily Furlong of Bell Street, Maidenhead and Tom Hunt of No.74 Grenfell Road, and at its peak the little fleet is said to have numbered three buses, indicating that other vehicles remain unaccounted for.

Apparently Mr. Tuck and Mrs. Furlong were 'on very friendly terms', and she was virtually running the bus service, the pair later living together in Maidenhead. She is also recalled by a regular passenger for her habit of stopping the bus on the afternoon run at The New Inn at Battle Bridge (since re-named as the Three Legged Cross, now an Indian Restaurant) for a 'swift half', whilst the passengers sat in the bus outside! The earliest known timetable of 20th February 1924 is as shown in the Maidenhead Advertiser, on the next page, the Hinds Head being at the top of the High Street.

Indeed, such was the popularity of the link that a letter in the Maidenhead Advertiser of 10th September 1924 praised the 'little yellow buses and their male and female drivers' for their service and the associated link for parcels. During the following month an appeal in that same journal sought an evening service into Maidenhead for those wishing to attend the cinema, something which proved a tonic during the long Winter months, and that was provided, though perhaps only on certain days. Back in August the Bracknell Sports Day had seen frequent departures from Maidenhead throughout the day for that popular event.

As already noted, the vehicles used by *Bob Tuck* are incomplete in details, as the second Ford (MO 2060) was with another owner from 30th March 1926, and the original Ford (BL 7814) had gone to *H.J. Beasley* of Windsor as a bus from January to April 1928.

When the *Yellow Bus Service* started there was no competition over the road to Bracknell, and although the *Blue Bus Service* operated by *West Bros.* of Bray also used the Braywick Road, it then turned off to the village. At Jealotts Hill an experimental agricultural research farm had been set up, which developed into Nitrams Ltd., and the latter had a need for a bus service at times suitable to the working day. As that was not catered for by the shopping-orientated *Mustard Pot*, that firm had approached the *Thames Valley Traction Co. Ltd.* in April 1928. In its response the *'Valley* noted that it would need to consider purchasing the *Yellow Bus Service* in order to provide an amended timetable, and would want Nitrams to pay 50% of that cost, whilst also indemnifying it against any operating loss on the service. It clearly did not reckon much on the viability of such a link!

Much earlier on the *Great Western Railway* had pioneered its bus service from Maidenhead to Holyport in May 1912, but had withdrawn it in July 1914. However, in April 1928 it re-opened a Road Motor's centre in the town, causing it to examine the local

competition. Apparently, it was not keen to run through to Bracknell, as there was mutual suspicion between itself and the *Southern Railway,* which had a railway station there. The exact date of the takeover of the *Yellow Bus Service* has not been discovered, and the start date of the *GWR* service recorded as 2nd July 1928 is some weeks after it had been noted by Maidenhead BC that the service had changed hands. As the other route out of Maidenhead to Littlewick Green and Twyford commenced operation on 2nd April 1928, it is possible that was in fact when the take-over took effect.

However, the *GWR* decided not to run beyond Jealotts Hill, and also to take in Bray village, which put it in direct conflict with *West Bros.* The latter responded to that, and the loss of the Bracknell link, by extending its service to the latter town from Wednesday 25th April 1928, which provides further evidence that the chocolate and cream railway buses were indeed already in operation. These moves by the *Great Western* also had the effect of ending the talks between *Thames Valley* and Nitrams, and resulted in the latter (now as Imperial Chemical Industries) actually buying a pair of Hoyal-bodied Guy OND 20-seater buses (RX 6849/50) in May 1930 for such use!

The regular pony-racing and steeplechase meetings at Hawthorn Hill saw some significant additional traffic, which the railway was well-placed to issue through facilities in respect of longer-distance travellers, but otherwise it was principally interested in providing feeder services to its rail services from Maidenhead, so the *Blue Bus* now became the sole means for reaching Bracknell. On the other hand, in due course the share-holdings of the *GWR* and the *Southern* in *Thames Valley* would inevitably lead both of them to periodically consider the need for a through route from Maidenhead to Bracknell. Although it inherited the Jealotts Hill service from the *Great Western* in September 1931, *Thames Valley* was not particularly enthusiastic about the route, which was even less profitable using a crew-operated 32-seat Tilling-Stevens than with the previous one-man 14-seater Morris-Commercial which came with the route. The subsequent history of the services between the towns of Bracknell and Maidenhead took quite a few twists and turns, whilst the provision of transport for workers at the Jealotts Hill Research Station was met by contracts for much of the time, instead of forming part of a more viable service operation, all of which appear in greater detail under the heading of *West Bros & Bray Transport* in this volume.

The little yellow buses were remembered with affection for many years after their demise, for the way they brightened up the local lanes, and indeed the lives of the villagers. After the sale *Bob Tuck* could be found living in Grenfell Road, Maidenhead along with Emily Furlong, though he took no further part in the local public transport scene, working as a decorator and painter.

Albert Edward Warwick
Warwick Bus Service
Farnham Common and Maidenhead

Albert had been born at Nutfield in Surrey in 1897, living at No.6 Peyton Cottages, though by 1911 the family was in Alton, Hampshire. By 1915 he was employed as a chauffeur-mechanic, though living with his mother at Waterloo Farm back in Surrey at Horsley. He enlisted at Grove Park for the Army Service Corps Mechanical Transport Section in March 1915, duly going over to France in July to drive in the Ammunition Supply Unit, though latterly he was with a Mobile Repair Unit up to his demobilisation in June 1919, his address then as No.22 Queens Road in South Norwood. On his return he married Audrie Brocq, and we hear nothing more of him until 1929.

In June 1929, in company with his brother *J. Warwick* (he had brothers John and Joe), they obtained a small charabanc under the title *Warwick Bros.,* though by 1931 Albert was on his own with the enterprise. More developments followed, but all were centred on his new home area of Farnham Common, involving Windsor and Slough, so out of the scope of this volume. That part of his history is already available in *London Buses Volume 3 by Blacker, Lunn & Westgate*, so we shall only concern ourselves with his Maidenhead area activities, which got his attention after the new *London Passenger Transport Board* bought his bus operations on Saturday 27th October 1934.

This Morris-Commercial Z6-type (RX 5738) had been supplied by Hewen's Garage of Maidenhead, and it had semi-luxury seats and a sun-shine roof, so it could be used on private hire work as well. It was seen bearing the fleet number 3 in King Street, Maidenhead on a short-working to Tittle Row. Note the timetable folders in the window, also that Carter's Booking Office is to its rear at No.119.

As it was, other local operators of some years standing were then thinking about their futures, so it was not long before *Bert Warwick* found some wanting to sell. Messrs *Fuller & Pomroy* had started to dispose of their

operations, as otherwise they would have needed to buy some more modern vehicles. They had started in 1926, having sold one service to *Thames Valley* in 1933, so they now disposed of the Maidenhead to Hurley route, along with excursions and tours licenses in March 1935, the booking office at No.107 Queen Street also being taken over, but no vehicles were involved. The *Beta Bus Services* fleet was time-expired, so *Warwick* obtained an interesting little Guy 'Victory' (MY 4117) to cover the service from June 1935, having used a 1929 Morris-Commercial 16-seater (RX 5738) he had transferred from Slough in the interim.

Although small, the little Guy was in fact a forward-control ONDF-type with a United body seating 20. It was one of a pair, both of which were new in 1930 to Royal Highlander, passing to Loumax, then to London General. They had a 4-cylinder 3.3-litre Meadows petrol engine, and LGOC placed them in store for 2 years, so Warwick acquired his in June 1935.

He also needed to assemble a small coaching fleet quite rapidly to continue the usual round of excursions and private hire, particularly as he had in the interim also acquired the licenses of *Walter Freemen* of Windsor (*Windsor Castle Coaches*) which gave him a range of excursions starting from Langley. He transferred an existing Bedford WLB coach (AKX 786) of 1934 with 20-seater Duple body, and also his January 1935 WLB with similar body (JB 5209), those bearing the fleet numbers 1 and 2, though any others are unconfirmed other than the Morris 3 by its photo evidence. The name *Warwick Sunsaloon Coaches* now came into use.

To supplement them he added in August 1935 a well-travelled ADC 424-type coach with Duple 24-seater body (RU 6734), new in July 1928 to *Elliott Bros.* (*Royal Blue*) of Bournemouth, which had passed with some of that firm to *Hants & Dorset* in February 1935, though they did not make use of it, selling it on to a dealer. To complete the line up at Maidenhead, in July 1935 he acquired another coach with numerous former owners, as a Gilford 166OT-type of 1929 with a 26-seater body also by United of Lowestoft (VX 2262), and his base was by then at No.31 Marlow Road.

The ADC 424-model came from a period when AEC and Daimler co-operated to produce chassis using the best of their respective expertise, the Daimler engine being quiet in operation, and RU 6734 was one of a batch of 26 bought by Elliott's for their coach fleet.

By 1936 that site was referred to as the Warwick Coaching Station, with petrol sales also available there. In the meantime, back in April 1935 he had managed to add an express service from Maidenhead to Bognor Regis and Littlehampton, which operated on Saturdays and Sundays from 1st July to 30th September. However, for the following year he requested an increase to a daily operation, but that was successfully opposed by *Carter's* and *Thames Valley*, so was refused.

He had in fact increased his hold on the local coach scene, when the long-established *Harry Clinch* decided to sell his *Maidonian Coaches* to *Warwick* in August 1935, the existing license having 12 destinations. So, as can be seen, in quite rapid succession *Bert Warwick* had re-established himself at Maidenhead, by taking over the activities of *Freeman, Fuller & Pomroy* and *Clinch*, looking set to build further upon that.

However, perhaps all was not as well as it appeared, as on 5th April 1936 he accepted an offer from *Thames Valley* to buy his Maidenhead to Hurley service, as they had now acquired the pair of Maidenhead to Henley links with the *Ledbury Transport* transfer. And then, during September and October 1936 his various Road Service Licenses were all surrendered! That in respect of the Langley excursions was taken up by *E. J. Sargeant* of Slough (*Slough Coaching Service*), who also bought the Bedford WLB JB 5209 for further use.

Quite what prompted the sudden demise of what looked like a promising enterprise is unclear, though perhaps the cost of assembling the local fleet was not being recovered quickly enough? By 1939 the couple were to be found running the Rising Sun pub at Milland, a small village south of Liphook on the Hampshire and West Sussex border, the Register of that year noting him as Motor Mechanic now Licensed Victualler, along with his army pension, and he passed away in that area during 1982.

West Bros.
Westward Ho Bus Service, Blue Bus Service, Bray Transport Ltd.
Bray, Berkshire

Passenger transport from the Thames riverside village of Bray was in the hands of the same family for some 5 decades, though they were far from natives of the area.

Indeed, we must first look to the Gloucestershire area of Tetbury, and the small hamlet of Chavenage Green in order to study their backgrounds. At 1911 the family was headed by William West, who was a coachman at Chavenage House, though he had originated in Melton in Norfolk, whilst his wife came from Doncaster in the South Riding of Yorkshire. Their eldest daughter had been born in Yorkshire in 1890, but all the others were local births, with eldest son Frederick born in 1892, but they, along with the youngest child Alice, will play no further part in our story. However, it is sons John William (aged 16 and a domestic groom), Joseph Alfred (age 13), Stephen George (age 9) and Martin Edward (age 6) that we will encounter again.

Quite soon after that John (known as 'Jack') decided to emigrate to Canada to get away from life as a servant, working on the Canadian Pacific Railway. With the outbreak of the Great War, he enlisted in the Army and was posted to the 16th Canadian Scottish Regiment and rose to Acting Corporal by 1917, when he was injured in Flanders. From there he was shipped to England to recover at the Canadian Red Cross Hospital set in the grounds of the Astor estate at Cliveden, a few miles north-east of Maidenhead and on the Buckinghamshire bank of the River Thames. Whilst convalescing there he met Edith Clara Norsworthy, daughter of a long-standing Bray family, resulting in their marriage on 31th July 1917.

Ans so it was that the Great War not only saw the return of Jack to his native England, but placed him at Bray, where he started to consider his future employment. He obtained a large old Renault car, which could seat 8 persons, and with that he commenced a taxi service to Maidenhead, some 2 miles away, plus other hires to meet trains at the Station there, or to local events such as Ascot Races and the regattas held along the River. At first the car was kept in the garage of the Hinds Head Hotel in the centre of the village, whilst the couple lived with her parents at No.3 The Homestead, close by.

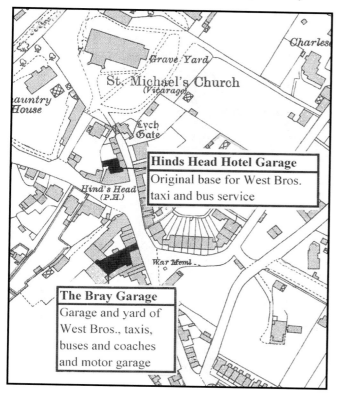

Hinds Head Hotel Garage
Original base for West Bros. taxi and bus service

The Bray Garage
Garage and yard of West Bros., taxis, buses and coaches and motor garage

The taxi soon attracted a number of regular clients, and some villagers got together to share rides into the town for shopping and other attractions such as the cinema, as although the *British Automobile Traction Co. Ltd.* was developing further services, it showed no interest in serving the village as such. So, in late 1919 brother Steve came up and the Renault became the *Westward Ho Bus Service*, the title alluding to Jack's earlier departure for the New World. Steve also started to develop garage services for the growing numbers of private motorists, which in due course would become the main thrust of his business energies, whilst Martin (Ted) followed in 1922/3, at the age of 18.

The Renault was at times over-subscribed, so it was decided to buy a proper bus, in the shape of a new Chevrolet B-type with 14-seater rear-entrance bus body, which arrived in April 1924 as MO 3096. It was initially licensed by Jack and, as it bore a livery of blue, the venture now became the *Blue Bus Service*. A very similar bus followed in March 1925, initially licensed to Ted, though both became *West Bros.* at renewals. They were followed by a Morris T-type bus in May

1925, which had a 14-seater front-entrance bus body and had been supplied complete by H.E. Hewens, the Maidenhead-based agent for Morris. At that point the old Renault was retired, plus the first non-family driver was employed as Jim Aitken, who stayed for some years, but by 1939 had gone heavy lorry-driving for Pickford's Removals in Bell Street at Maidenhead.

Despite the known details as outlined above, there was no record of formal licensing of the service until June 1923, when Maidenhead BC issued a hackney carriage license, so it seems likely that prior to that the service had used a private yard, as the carriers often did. The base at Bray remained the Hinds Head Hotel. Indeed, it seems possible the Council had been alerted by the first known advert in the Advertiser, dated 23rd May, which showed that the bus left Bray at 8am, 10am, 11am, 2.15pm, 3.15pm, 4.30pm and 6pm, returning from Maidenhead at 9am, 10.45am, 12noon, 2.30pm, 4pm, 5pm and 7.30pm. It also stated that private parties could be catered for, apply Mr. Collins, tobacconist No.42 Grenfell Road, which was close by the Station. Family sources also confirm that originally there was not a Sunday service, so excursions to the South Coast ran.

The British Empire Exhibition at Wembley was a great success for 1924, being revived and enhanced for a 1925 season as well. As the family settled into the new business, Ted had been lodging with Jack and Edith, but in 1928 he married Ivy Bailey, so they set up home at 'Adrienne' in Holyport, though later they relocated to 'Capstan' on the Holyport Road. Stephen, on the other hand, was the only brother not to marry, and he continued to reside at No.1 Oldfield Cottages and was instrumental in developing the Bray Garage. Indeed, the original use of the Hinds Head Garage had needed to be supplemented by a bus parked at The Vicarage and another in a barn behind Bray Cottage, so in 1927 they purchased Thames House, which faced onto the High Street, with a large yard and garden area through its large wooden gates. Petrol pumps were set up on the pavement, then in due course the 4 old cottages at the rear were purchased and demolished. By 1930 a large wooden shed had been erected over the site of the old sunken garden. Just to complete the story, that shed was used during WW2 as an engineering facility to prepare parts for tanks and aircraft, one of many such locations. In 1969 the final phase saw the frontage of Thames House become a car showroom for the Bray Garage.

In the meantime, the bus service was found to require further capacity, so a 20-seater front-entrance Guy OW-type was purchased in June 1927 as RX 329. It was followed in June 1928 by another 20-seater with front entrance on a Bean Model 11 chassis as RX 2558, the body by Metcalfe and being painted two shades of brown, must be assumed to be an off-the-peg purchase

The little Guy bus was the only purchase of that make, but it remained in service until September 1938, and is seen on Station Approach at Maidenhead. Note the ad board for 'Macadam gave us good roads, give me OXO for good health'.

from a dealer. It had smart red leather seating and came just in time for the busy Royal Ascot Race Week. It was, however, duly repainted blue and cream, but after the new Construction & Use Regulations of 1931, its inward-facing seats over the wheel-arches were turned and its capacity reduced to 18. It is also recalled for having very powerful headlights that shone for miles!

It seems the rear-entrance Chevrolets were both duly retired with the above arrivals, though initially retained as spare buses to 1930/1. Further drivers joining around then were Freddie Wooster of No.1 Warren View in Holyport, Fred Thatcher of No.30 Portlock Road in Maidenhead, and Bill Smallbone of No.2 Woodbine Cottages in Hibbert Road in the village. With such steady employment, and in preference to agricultural work, many of the employees racked up many years of loyal service. Also, although not a carrier's service as such, drivers often did errands for villagers, such as collecting medicines or taking accumulators to be re-charge, plus a regular order on Friday evenings for fish'n'chip suppers collected from Pomroy's shop in Grenfell Road!

Indeed, at this juncture we can benefit from some of the recollections of Bill's son Len Smallbone, who the author interviewed in the 1990's. Apart from details of the other employees and individual vehicles, he told me

of Jack's rather lucrative side-line as an unofficial book-maker, then a commonplace situation in fact, and Bill often did the 'running' to place the bets whilst the bus was laid over, Jack giving him a share of the commission. He reckoned Jack made more that way than from the bus service. Now Bill usually drove the Bean, bringing it home at night to park at the end of their road at the Braywick end. One year the family had a week off to go to Bognor Regis, so he arranged with Jack to borrow the bus, most seats were removed and they all 'camped out' in it! During the 1940's there was a fire at the garage, so young Len, who was in the yard, jumped in a bus and drove it to safety, despite never having driven before, though often accompanying his father in the school holidays. Bill stayed until the end of operations in 1969 and then retired.

An advert for excursions in July 1927 shows that at that point some at least started from the Bell Hotel, near the Railway Station in Maidenhead, with a Brighton trip departing at 7.30am for a 10 shillings fare. However, local competition soon convinced the bothers to stay more local, picking up in Bray, Holyport, Money Row Green, Touchen End and Paley Street only after that.

On the bus service, several other local developments were instrumental in seeing its expansion, so we must first understand the background. Since August 1923 *Robert Tuck* of Touchen End had run his *Yellow Bus* between Maidenhead and Bracknell, but he did not deviate into Bray, so no competition with *Blue Bus* had ensued. Also, by the Spring of 1928, the Nitrams Research Farm at Jealotts Hill was expanding, with its experimental use of nitrogen-based fertilisers to aid yield-rates for crops. It had approach *Thames Valley* to see if that operator could provide a better bus service, seeking links to Maidenhead and to Bracknell for the transport of its workers. *TV's* Board considered that in order to make that a paying proposition it would need to remove the competition from the *Yellow Bus*, and in order to do that, would require a 50% contribution from Nitrams, resulting in no conclusion as such.

At virtually the same time of those discussions, the *Great Western Railway* had decided to re-open a *Road Motors* location at Maidenhead to develop its own services, which led it to consider purchasing *Yellow Bus* to remove it from competition. That approach took place in April 1928, with a takeover date of May quoted by one source, though the timings may not be correct. As although the *Road Motors* service did not commence until 2nd July 1928, *Jack West* had cause to complain to Maidenhead BC in May that, despite his own service being approved by them, they had allowed the Railway Company to divert what now became a Maidenhead to Jealotts Hill service through Bray!

And so it was, that from Wednesday 25th April 1928 the *Blue Bus* extended its service through to Bracknell! It should, of course, be noted that prior to that the bus route had developed to local points beyond Bray, with journeys reaching Holyport, Money Row Green, Sturt Green, Touchen End and Paley Street. It is of course interesting to note that the *GWR* paid to buy *Tuck* out, but failed to capitalise on having a link to the market town of Bracknell, but it has been said it did not want to upset the Southern Railway by appearing there? As it was, the route to Jealotts Hill would never pay. In due course the Railway bought shares in *Thames Valley*, which inherited the service in September 1931, but also failed to make any money over that road!

Although that provided a useful link for locals between those two towns, it did not satisfy the needs of Nitram employees for travel to the Jealotts Hill site, so that firm, which had become part of the Imperial Chemical Industries group, decided to provide its own buses! For that role it purchased a pair of Guy OND's fitted with 20-seater bus bodies by Hoyal of Weybridge, which took to the road as RX 6849/50 in May 1930. One bus ran from Maidenhead Station and the other started out from Bracknell Station at suitable times, that private operation continuing until late in 1937, after which it was decided to have contracted vehicles instead.

Another new employee joining with the expansion of the garage in May 1928 was Jim Eiles, though he went onto the bus side from July, another driver who stayed through to 1969. For many years he had lived nearby at 'Crossways' in New Road, Holyport, and in 1931 he married Minnie Blackall, another established surname locally, of which we shall hear more of in due course.

Jim recalled the names of his other contemporaries in the 1930's onwards as the former *Thames Valley* man Fred Quelch of Maidenhead, Sid Watts, Bill Hing who was an ex-RASC driver of the Great War who married a Bray girl to live at No.17 The Terrace, Ron Beckett, 'Darkie' Haines, Jack Kite of No.2 White Hart Cottages at Money Row Green, Charlie Creffield of No.65 Boyne Valley Road in Maidenhead and also Fred Curtain, so a significant local employer.

With the coming of the Road Traffic Act 1930, which took effect from 1st January 1931, the new system of licensing for services resulted in an application by *West Bros.* in May 1931 to continue the bus service from Grenfell Road in Maidenhead to the variety of termini already noted above, all of which were granted. At the same time an Excursions & Tours License was required for such work, for which a rather modest selection was requested, in fact just a half-day trip to the quite local beauty spot of Burnham Beeches, an evening excursion for the Aldershot Military Tattoo, Ascot Race Week, plus full-day coastal excursions to Bognor Regis and Brighton, also taking in Littlehampton and Worthing. All started from the Bray Garage and, although other pick-up points were not specifically requested, it was the case that passengers continued to be picked up at Holyport (The Green), Money Row Green (White Hart) and Touchen End (Hinds Head).

Whereas coaching work earlier had been carried out using a spare bus, the first dedicated coach-seated body was a fabric-sided Weymann-type 19-seater fitted to a Commer 'Invader' 6TK-type chassis as RX 9046, new in July 1931. However, it had been built for *Stanley Bros.* of Andover, coming to the *Wests* after that firm failed or had been taken over, so it carried a livery of cream and brown for some years.

The 14-seater Morris (MO 5307) remained in use until the close of 1935, but in the meantime several small Dennis buses were added, the secondhand market being awash with good stock due to various firms packing up or takeovers by Territorial Companies of independents.

From Wilts & Dorset came a Dennis similar to this one, a 30cwt with 18-seater body by Short Bros., which had been employed on chasing duties.

MW 1510 was one of a number of Dennis 30-cwt buses used by *Wilts & Dorset* for fighting competition, new in 1928 with a Short Bros. 18-seater bus body, arriving during 1935, whilst NF 9367 was a G-type with a 20-seater bus body, new in 1928 to *Sharpe's Bus Service* of Longsight, acquired at an unrecorded date.

The Dodge coach RD 5481 seen when new, with its well-appointed body, and also note the luggage area between the front wheel and the front entrance.

Operations then settled down to that pattern for the 1930's, although at some point the Maidenhead stop returned to the Station Approach, though only a short distance from Grenfell Road. The little Guy bus (RX 329) continued to give good service until March 1938, being finally broken up at the Garage during 1939. The 1931 Commer (RX 9046) was replaced around March 1939 by another of that make, but a forward-control 'Invader'-type fitted with a 24-seater coach body most likely built by Waveney. Registered RD 5481 it had been new to *G. Jarvis & Son of Reading (Reading & District Motor Services)* in 1934, passing to *Smith's Coaches* of Reading on the first day of 1936. RX 9046 was duly broken up by the firm at the Garage in 1939.

As with all other passenger operators, the *Blue Bus* now entered a war-footing from September 1939, with vehicles rushing off to move troops, evacuees and new shadow factories needing worker's transport, airfields and army camps being constructed, then in due course the transport of Prisoners of War on agricultural duties. The general shortage of vehicles saw a number of odd additions to the fleet, though none were requisitioned.

The Dennis 'Lancet' described in the next column.

The previous good relations with *Alf Smith* of Reading also helped in sourcing vehicles, as he had good connections with the dealer Arlington. Through that connection came one of a number of surplus coaches from the Isle of Wight, brought to the mainland by that dealer and offered to *Smith's Coaches*, an unusual normal-control Dennis 'Lancet' coaches with dark green-painted 26-seater Duple body new in May 1932 as DL 7908 to *Randall* of Ventnor, arriving in May 1941. That was followed by a Dodge with flamboyant fully-fronted bodywork by REAL Coachworks, new in June 1936 as RD 7766 to *A.C. Cox (Silver Grey)* of Reading, another firm to pass to *Smith's Coaches* in March 1939. That coach had been requisitioned, but was subsequently offered back to *Smith's*, but declined and its availability highlighted to *West Bros.* who got it in November 1941. Another coach which had served in the *Smith's* fleet was 1928 Lancia 'Pentaiota' YW 939, fitted with a London Lorries body that had been updated with a solid roof, sold to *Brimblecombe Bros.* of Wokingham by June 1941, who re-sold it to *Blue Bus* in December 1941. Such old coaches were of course useful on contracts where the vehicle did not return until the end of the day, or even longer periods.

Dodge RD 7766 is shown when new to Silver Grey.

Operation under wartime conditions saw difficult driving conditions in the black-out, another advantage in having local men who literally knew the lanes like the back-of-their-hands. The last run back to the camps in the area from Maidenhead often saw the big Dennis carrying over 50 passengers, and it proved reliable.

In respect of the bus service, an Emergency Timetable came into effect from 4th December 1939, which saw the route curtailed at Paley Street at its southern end. The pattern of termini in the local area continued much as before, having been honed to match local needs, but services ended earlier in the evening. A few journeys were now apparently routed out of Maidenhead via the High Street and to Bray along the 'Lower Road' past Avenue Road, and also in the opposite direction. There was still a Sunday service, with much the same pattern of journeys, surprisingly frequent in fact, which shows the importance of that link.

The Lancia YW 939 seen in its heyday with Smith's.

Now, as we have already seen, the Great War had been the catalyst responsible for the start of the bus service from Bray by Jack and, in due course, his brothers. By 1939 Jack and Edith had moved into 'Cosy Cottage', with one son John William (born 1918), and also 3 daughters, Kathleen Edith Betty (1922), Doreen Olive (1926) and Molly Evelyn Jean (1929), all still at home other than John, who was now across the road as a tobacconist. Living with the family was Edith's father William Swain Norsworthy, a 70-year old retired sign-writer, that must have been useful for lettering the fleet, plus as a lodger one of the taxi drivers, Bernard Shanks, who duly married daughter Kathleen. Next door at No.1 Oldfield Cottages was still Steve, that also being next to the Bray Garage.

John had already enlisted in the Territorials, so on the outbreak of war he went to the Royal Artillery, serving with an Ant-tank Unit as rear-guard in the evacuation of Dunkirk. During December 1942 he took part in the Allied Landings in North Africa and was unfortunately killed in action near Tunis. Others in the family did their bit, with Steve attached to the Auxillary Fire Service, whilst Joe was Flying Officer with the No.155 Maidenhead Air Defence Corps. Indeed, his continued involvement with the No.323ATC Gliding School at White Waltham as its Commanding Officer earned him the MBE in 1960.

The importance of the local operations was further acknowledged by the allocation of the Ministry of Supply for two of the famous Bedford OWB 'utility' buses, with CJB 352 arriving in July 1943 and CRX 344 following in December 1944, both with 32-seater bodies with wooden slatted seats.

The taxi business had continued alongside the other operations, and by the late 1940's about 3 Armstrong-Siddeley cars were in use, though later Wolseleys were instead favoured, whilst Jack's personal transport was a Buick 'Straight 6'. One of the other regular hires was

in connection with the popular dinner-dances hosted by the Hotel de Paris, which would see around 3 coaches bringing down waiting staff from London and back.

The first post-war purchase was a Bedford OB-type with Mulliner bus body seating 30, which arrived in April 1948 as EJB 271, which was followed by a similar 28-seater in June 1949 (FBL 515), and they led to the withdrawal of the Dodge (RD 7766) and the Dennis 'Lancet' (DL 7908). Another Bedford OWB was acquired in December 1948 (BBW 331), in order to cover for a vehicle off the road due to accidental damage, purchased from *Kemp's MS* of Woodcote, as they were requiring larger capacity buses for post-war contracts such as AERE Harwell. Its original wooden seats as fitted when new in January 1943 had been replaced by 29 coach seats in the meantime.

Earlier it was mentioned that Fred Quelch had served with Thames Valley prior to spending the rest of his career with Blue Bus/Bray Transport, and here we see him with TV's Thornycroft charabanc Car 13 (DP 2129) on a church outing in the 1920's.

Within the four brothers, it was the founder Jack, along with Steve, who were the most business-minded, with Joe assisting in the garage and Ted with the passenger operations. So, it was decided to reform the outfit as *Bray Transport Ltd.*, with effect from 3rd May 1948, which also brought in *Ronald Herbert Leslie Blackall* into the frame. The Blackalls were another established Bray family, and he was in fact the cousin to Minnie Eiles, and with him came additional capital.

The license for the Maidenhead (Station) to Paley Street (Royal Oak) route was applied for to continue

The Bedford OWB's helped the firm continue through the war years, and they were rugged buses. Here we see CRX 344 ploughing through the local floods of 1947 on its way to Maidenhead.

under the new name when it came up for renewal in July 1948, and then from 4th April 1949 it was decided to reinstate the full route through to Bracknell again. As a matter of interest, there had been something of a campaign by those 'stranded' at Jealotts Hill through the Parish Council to get a bus service reinstated, there having been a small estate of houses built at that point for the workers at the Research Station. Although they could walk over to their allotted tasks, it was the wives that cried out for buses to undertake shopping etc. As a result of that several other operators had proposed services, including *Gough's Garage* of Bracknell, with a proposal for a route from Hawthorn Hill via Warfield. Fuller details will be found in the volume covering Bracknell, Crowthorne & Wokingham, but it was due to *Bray Transport's* reinstatement that the proposal by *Gough's* was duly modified to start from Warfield.

So the new firm start with a fleet comprising the trio of Bedford OWB's as BBW 331, CJB 352 and CRX 344, along with Bedford OB's EJB 271 and FBL 515, and with the early post-war economy being what it was, no additions were made for 4 years.

Replacements for the native OWB's came as further OB-types, in May 1954 (DFE 708) of 1949, and in March 1955 (GNM 976) of 1947, both with Duple 'Vista' 29-seater coach bodies. The first SB-series for the fleet followed in May 1956 as a 1953 petrol-engine SB-type with Burlingham 'Seagull' 35-seater body (FTK 250), the additional capacity necessary for a school contract to Maidenhead from the villages. May

1957 saw another OB-type with Duple 'Vista' 29-seater body (KCD 736) of 1950 added, then a similar coach followed in March 1958 (JNP 990) of the same vintage. That resulted in the withdrawal of the 1948/9 Mulliner-bodied OB buses, with EJB 271 departing in November 1958 and FBL 515 the following month. A trio of Duple 'Vega'-bodied Bedford SBO-types came in May 1958, with NOR 323 of 1955 with 38 seats and in November/December 1958 ASB 373/4 of 1954 and with 36 seats. After that there followed a succession of Bedford SB-series coaches, full details of which can be found on page 94. However, from the mid-1960's the fleet declined from 8 in 1964, 6 in 1965 and just 4 at the start of 1969, though only 2 were in operation.

Early post-war Bedford OB-type EJB 271 was often used on school runs, as evident in this photo, in company with another OB (JNP 990).

Mention has already been made of the contracting of transport by ICI in respect of the Jealotts Hill site, and in the meantime *Thames Valley* had for a while been covering the run from Maidenhead. However, by 1955 it was finding it difficult to find enough vehicles and drivers, so it was surrendered, being taken over from April 1955 by *Bray Transport*. It was a weekdays-only operation from Maidenhead (Station), but in January 1958 it increased to 2 vehicles.

In the meantime, the business lost its founder when Jack West passed away on 8th May 1954. His obituary notes his wide involvement in the local community, noting he was known as the 'Harbourmaster of Bray'. For the record, both Ted and Steve duly relocated to different locations in Somerset, passing away in 1998 and 2000 respectively, whilst Joe remained local and died in 1990.

OCO 169 was an SB1-type with Duple 'Vega' body new in 1958, seen approaching Epsom on Derby Day.

*A couple of Bedford coaches from the Bray Transport era, with **above** – 1959 SB3-type with Duple 'Super Vega' body (UOT 587), and **below** – 1958 example with 'Vega'-style body (UUF 535), the latter on hire to Beach's Coaches of Staines.*

As previously noted, the Bracknell route was never a great paying concern, and by June 1960 there were only three through journeys on weekdays, arriving there at 9.35am, 1.52pm and 5.10pm. All variants were now shown on a single timetable, which had developed to include schooldays timings to Braywick School from various points in and around Holyport and Bray. There was a service between Maidenhead and Paley Street on a Sunday, in fact with 14 varied journeys.

However, increases in operating costs were affecting all operators, large and small, as the 1960's wore on, so from 1st May 1961 the service was reduced to run as Maidenhead (Station) to Paley Street (Royal Oak), but still retained the established pattern of variations. The Sunday operation was abandoned from January 1964, whilst the Omnibus Society records that the route was shortened slightly to run via Sheepcote Lane at Paley Street at some point, which gave a more convenient means of turning without reversing, but the date has not been confirmed through licensing applications.

After more reductions in revenue, it was decided to sell the service route, and on 2nd March 1966 it was taken over by *Ron Cole*, grandson of *Albert Victor Cole*, who had since the 1920's operated from Windsor to Eton, Eton Wick, Dorney and Maidenhead, using the title *Blue Bus Service*! His father had recently sold the Maidenhead to Windsor service to *Thames Valley*, and on 31st October 1969 it also took over the Paley Street route, which was duly reinstated through to Bracknell once again as Route 14- another twist in the tale!

Bray Transport in its heyday, with Bedford OB-type coach JNP 990 on a service to Holyport, waiting departure on the forecourt of Maidenhead Station.

Following the sale of the bus service, *Bray Transport* continued with contracts and some private hire mostly generated by local schools, but by the end of 1968 the

Directors reached the conclusion that it could not go on, so the goodwill of the work-in-hand was sold to the Maidenhead-based *Walwyn Coaches*, which had started in a small way with a minibus in 1959, taking that title from July 1962. No vehicles were involved, and all were duly sold off direct from Bray, the garage side continuing for many more years.

And lastly, a couple of reminders of significant times in the long history of Blue Bus and its successor Bray Transport.

One of the longest-running buses was the little Guy OW-type purchased in 1927, which stayed through to September 1938! Under Construction & Use it needed to have its oil-lamps replaced by electric ones, and also a guard-rail was fitted. Behind it in this photo on Station Approach is The To & Fro Cycle Company.

The re-instatement of the route through to Bracknell in 1949 was the first that many locals realised the firm had also been re-formed as Bray Transport. A new proposal by Gough's Garage of Bracknell had envisaged a link by them from Hawthorn Hill, which seemed to have spurred Bray onto returning to that road, though it was never much of an earner as a service.

*Two adverts to accompany the following Lorry-charas of Maidenhead section, with **above** – July 1921 with Gibbons, and **below** – for Tom Nicholson and his bus The Dell, cashing in on traffic to Wembley for the British Empire Exhibition in 1924.*

Lorry-charabancs from Maidenhead, Berkshire

> Whilst the lorry-chara was by no means unique to the Maidenhead area, a number of localised factors saw its brief inclusion to a higher degree than evident elsewhere in the Thames valley.

As local haulage businesses went over to motors, or were formed from new after the Great War, it was only natural that their owners would look to the nearby War Department Slough Dump, some 4 miles to the east along the busy Bath Road, as a source of cheap vehicles. Added to that there were several important annual events based close to the town, with the Henley Regatta and Ascot Races drawing large crowds then, and for many years virtually anything with wheels had been used at such peak times. Many of these trips were organised through public houses or other clubs, often rather male-dominated, with comfort being not of paramount importance over having a good time at a reasonable cost.

As it was, conventional charabanc operations in that early post-war period were rather slower to get off the ground in the town than when compared with Reading and Newbury, the other towns of comparable size. The *British Automobile Traction Co. Ltd.* had fielded charas since the 1919 season in a limited way, but again did not really get going until 1921, by which time the local branch had become the *Thames Valley Traction Co. Ltd.* And so we find for a couple of seasons, advertised excursions being operated by motor lorries fitted with bench seats, whilst weather-proofing was in the form of a canvas tilt, if anything was actually available.

Frederick George Hill - H&H Garage

Frederick Hill was born in 1890 in West London, and by 1911 his father of the same name was licensee of the Stag & Hounds, a pub at the Bray end of Braywick Road, which ran through to Maidenhead Station. At that time young Fred was employed as a motor driver with someone locally, so was already experienced with such vehicles.

The first we hear of his activities is in the Maidenhead Advertiser of 20th June 1920, when haulage work was advertised using his home address of 'Cambera', on the Braywick Road. Early in 1921 he opened up the *H&H Garage,* which was on Braywick Road, nearby the railway bridge, and had cars and lorries for hire, in addition to facilities for the general motorist. The name is suggestive of a partner, and it is believed that the other person was his probably father, who may have helped his son set up in those times of unemployment.

This business is only involved with lorry-chara operations in respect of the June 1921 Ascot Races, when he ran his motor lorry with seats at 6 shillings return, along with a private 4-seater car on the four days of racing. The public trips started from the garage, but were not repeated after that event.

S. & A.E. Gibbons

The Gibbons family had an involvement with road haulage going back still further, whilst they were also active with passenger-carrying for somewhat longer. By 1911 High Wycombe-born 46-year-old *Samuel Gibbons* was living at No.40 Rutland Road in Maidenhead and was operating as a road contractor. His two sons were both born at Maidenhead, and they were *Sidney Samuel* (1891) and *Albert Edward* (1895). In 1911 they were working in the town respectively as coal hawker and an apprentice motor engineer.

Both of the sons saw war service, though Sidney's records have not survived. Albert went to Bulford Camp on Salisbury Plain in March 1915, and served in the 1096th MT Company of the Army Service Corps in various locations before his return in May 1919. We shall return to Sidney's post-war activities shortly, but when Albert returned the scene was set for a partnership between him and his father as motor hauliers and furniture removers, and the initial advert of 2nd June 1920 states they had 2-ton lorries available. The same advert also states that they would run their motor lorries to Ascot Races, departing from outside the Railway Station by the Clock Tower at 11.30pm, with a return fare of 7 shillings. Seats could be booked at No.40 Rutland Road or at 'The Gables' No.10 All Saints Avenue, which was where Albert and his wife Violet were now residing.

However, unlike *Fred Hill,* this was not a venture solely for the races, as the 'comfortable 20-seater motor lorry' was again advertised for a trip to Brighton (65 miles) on Sunday 4th July, and departed from the Clock Tower at 7.30am. It was also noted that other such trips would follow, and the 20-seater is again noted as running to Eastbourne (87 miles) on Sunday 25th July 1920, departing from the same point at 7am and with a fare of 15 shillings 6 pence, all slightly cheaper than the competition.

In the 'For Sale' columns of the Reading Mercury on 21st August 1920 Gibbons offered a 1916 Napier lorry of 3 tons, along with a 30-45cwt tipper-lorry of that same make new in 1919, but this could have been in the capacity of re-sale after purchasing vehicles from the nearby Slough Disposals Sales. Another Napier known was LT 8458, which was licensed as hackney and goods, including an optional 20-seater charabanc body, which was last licensed in December 1921.

For 1921 the advertised excursions commence from June, with Brighton on Sunday 5th, leaving from the Clock Tower at 7.30am, returning from the coast at

5.30pm, all for 13s 6d, whilst on the following Sunday there is an afternoon trip to Oxford (33 miles), departing from the corner of Marlow Road at 2.30pm for 6s return. The Derby at Epsom racecourse (40 miles) and the usual Ascot Races 4-day event are also catered for, with Ascot now reduced to 6 shillings.

Brighton, Oxford and Southsea (65 miles) excursions are all operated during July, with the same start points as used before, but the Sandown Races outing on Monday 1st August left from the White Horse Hotel Yard at 11am and cost 8 shillings. However, the advert for the latter specified that 20 passengers would be required for it to run. The season continued with another Oxford afternoon trip, finishing with Southsea on 7th August, there being no further adverts that year.

However, the haulage adverts did continue, and that of 24th August 1921 featured 'the fleet', and showed a 2-tonner and two 3-tonners with military-style lorry bodies and canvas tilts, all looking like ex-WD types, though the filmed copy makes identification difficult, one is certainly a Napier. The vehicles bear the legend *Gibbons & Gibbons,* though the adverts refer to *S. & A.E. Gibbons*, and unfortunately no good print of this has come to light.

Although the term charabanc does creep into the final advert of the 1921 season, there is no evidence that a specific chara-style body was in use. Indeed, when they return for the 1922 season, it is with the 20-seater lorry-chara for Ascot Races in June. Apart from two trips to Brighton on Saturday 17th June and Thursday 6th July, there were no other advertised excursions by them in 1922, which is no doubt due to developments by other to provide more custom-built vehicles. Also, for the 1922 outings only the All Saints Avenue address is used for making bookings. For 1923 the only instance of their involvement is for the Ascot Races in June, when they ran daily from the Wesleyan Church at the further reduced fare of 4s 6d, after which passenger work ceased altogether.

Sidney Samuel Gibbons

Whereas his brother Albert had returned from the Great War to work with their father, *Sidney Gibbons* re-established his existing coal and coke merchant's business by early 1921, although he lived very close by his parents at No.32 Rutland Road, Maidenhead. If he used a motor vehicle pre-war is not known, but on 22nd July 1921 he registered a former WD Daimler 22hp lorry as BL 8937, no doubt acquired from the Slough Disposal Sales. This green-painted vehicle was also noted in registration documents as being used with 20 seats, though no advertisements were placed in the local paper. It is likely that he did use it for a season or two, probably for private parties and sports teams, but during 1923 it was reclassified for goods only, the trade he continued in for some years.

George Edward Howard

George Howard was another Maidenhead coal dealer, who was established by 1920, and was based at No.9 Cromwell Road. On 20th May 1921 he put a new Ford Model T 1-tonner on the road as BL 8599, and which he declared as a lorry fitted with 14 portable seats when not carrying goods. As there are no recorded excursions operated by him, it is likely that this saw use mainly for local private hires for sports teams and clubs, once the coal-dust was swept out! It is later noted as goods only, and with him at his revised address of Courthouse Road, still as a coal merchant.

Reginald Stafford Hayman, Thomas Nicholson and John Franklin

The final gentleman to consider under this category was also a coal and coke merchant, as well as a haulage contractor, based at the Post Office in Boyn Hill Road on the western side of Maidenhead.

Reginald Stafford Hayman had been born in 1891/2 at Nailsworth in Gloucestershire, the son of a Great Western Railway signalman, so the family was at the parish of Great & Little Hampton, near Pershore, Worcestershire in 1901. By 1911 he was employed as a domestic footman, living at Portman Mews, off of Baker Street, Marylebone, London. When he enlisted in the army in December 1915, he and his mother were already at the Boyn Hill Post Office, after which he served in the Labour Corps until returning demobbed in January 1919.

Little is known of his passenger-carrying activities, though on 3rd May 1920 he registered a Maxwell 18hp lorry as BL 7233. It was described as a platform lorry with canopy on hoop sticks, in a dark blue livery with red lining, with 14 seats, presumably removed when used for goods. His only known newspaper advert was in respect of an excursion to Brighton on August Bank Holiday 1923, for the rather low price of 7s 6d (only half the cost of most others), and the same ad notes he had private cars for hire, as well as the other established aspects of the business.

However, he sold out to *Thomas Nicholson* in February 1924, who in turn went into partnership with *John Franklin* in a variety of transport and other types of business. Whether the sale included the Maxwell, and therefore continuation of its use in that form is not clear, as nothing further is heard of it on motor tax records until February 1929, when it was with another Boyn Hill owner as a goods vehicle. Similarly, the only vehicle known with *Nicholson* was a Morris (RX 3010) registered in September 1928, but without any record of its type and category of use.

The situation is also slightly complicated by the adoption of a name for the passenger exploits of *Tom*

Nicholson, known as *The Dell,* which certainly suggests something more akin to a dedicated vehicle rather than a lorry, and it is certainly noted in several adverts as a 'motor bus' from June 1924 onwards.

The initial ventures by this vehicle see it used for Ascot Races, leaving The Crown in Boyn Hill at 10.30am for the low fare of 4 shillings return. However, the real money-spinner of that year was the British Empire Exhibition at the new Wembley complex in North London, which included a five-ring circus, and in many places it was soon found that demand actually outstripped local operator's capacity. Such excursions were advertised at 9am from Boyn Hill Post Office every Monday and Thursday from 23rd April at a fare of 4 shillings, with children going for half-price. The advertisement also noted that private parties could be taken to that event on other days, at the same fares with a minimum of 10 persons. In addition, *Tom Nicholson* had lorries for hire, undertook household removals and was a coal and coke merchant from his base at Boyn Hill Post Office. Similar adverts continue through May and June 1924, with 'other runs arranged at moderate terms' for *The Dell.*

However, there are no further such passenger outings noted for 1924, which probably shows how much local competition was now evident, and for October 1924 a weekly carrier's service to London had been started. The following month it was announced that he had gone into partnership with *John Franklin,* and was transferred to No.1 Broadway in the centre of town. The full range of facilities covered the haulage of stone, sand, gravel, soil, turf and manure, as well as coal and coke and household removals. By 1929 the above had gone their separate ways, with *Franklin* still at No.1 Broadway as a cabinet-maker and furniture dealer and *Nicholson* now at No.3 The Colonnade as a fruiterer.

Albert Henry Wray

Wray was another local haulage contractor attempting charabanc operation briefly. He had been born in 1876, and in 1881 is found at Squirries Street in Bethnal Green, East London, living with his parents. In 1901 he was at No.4 Little Union Place in Stepney, and as in 1891 he was an apprentice carpenter to his father of that trade. He married Elizabeth Seabrook in August 1898 at Bethnal Green, and he was then a Police Constable. By 1911 the couple and three children were living with her brother at No.15 Boyn Hill Road in Maidenhead, and for some reason, at that point in time, he was using the name George Green! Confirmation of his identity comes from the presence of the couple still there in 1935/6, confirmed from other known facts.

In the meantime, he had joined the Royal Engineers in August 1915, serving in Egypt and rising to Sergeant. We next find him in 1924 as a haulage contractor, with a weekly carrier's service from Maidenhead area to London. That is further developed by his Directory entry for 1928, which shows *A.H. Wray & Co.,* with motor haulage, removals, coal and coke merchant and well-appointed motor charabanc. As his son A.H.W. Wray had been born in 1903, and is noted in 1939 as a bus driver locally, it must be assumed he had joined his father in the business as it developed. The address of No.63 Queen Street was given for the business, but the private residence remained at No.15 Boyn Hill Road. The offering of the charabanc was only for that one season, probably making use of a chassis used at other times for the also largely seasonal coal trade. The next known reference to him comes in 1939, still sat that same address, but now as a coach driver, though for which operator is not known. His son Albert is also still local, now as a bus driver, and also as a Wartime Special Police Constable.

An interesting tail-piece to the Early Independents of the Bracknell, Crowthorne & Wokingham Area

Following publication of the previous volume several interesting items came to light regarding the *Crimson Rambler* fleet, so now we can review them here. The first is an advert in Commercial Motor of 31st August 1926 for 3 Daimler 28-seater charabancs fitted with pneumatic tyres at £250 each, sale stated to be 'in the interest of standardisation, been working daily'. That was repeated on 21st September, adding a Sunbeam 14-seater charabanc for disposal.

Now, though it may just be coincidental, over at Reading in early 1926 a local motorist sold his 1914 Hotchkiss (BL 1351) car to Vincents Garage. In an interview with Henry House, he recalled how one brother of *House Bros.* of Watlington returned home one day with the chara shown below, mounted on that same Hotchkiss, much to the annoyance of his brother! As the use of the name Crimson Rambler has no place in the history of that operator, was it perhaps a body acquired and re-mounted by Vincents, that had originated from Teddington? It is seen about to leave Watlington, apparently on a service journey with Henry acting as boy conductor in school cap and with Bell Punch machine!

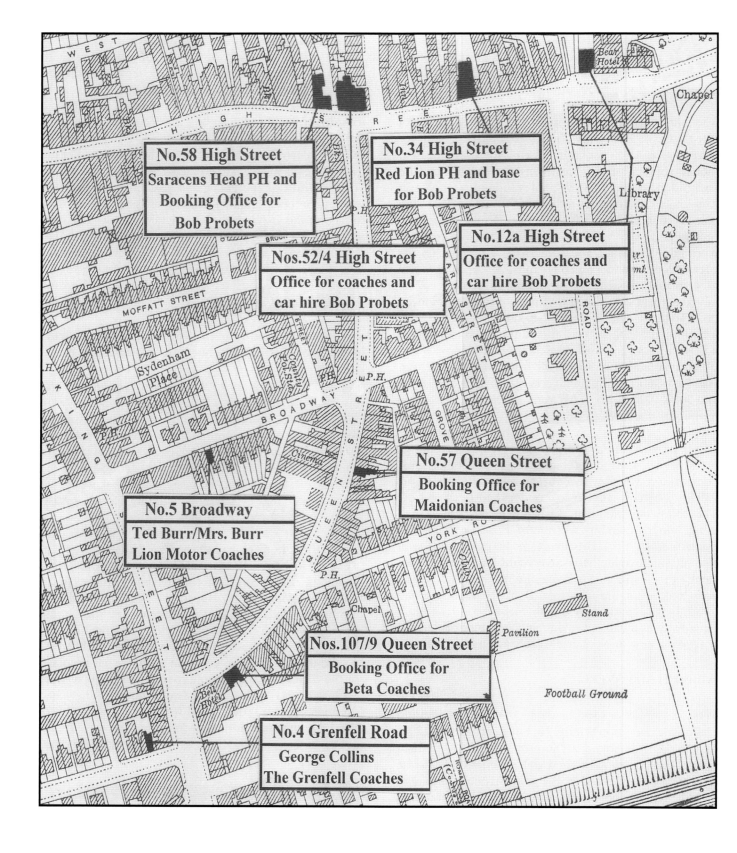

Location Map of Maidenhead Town Centre showing various points referred to under the headings for operators in this volume. A separate map for the Bell Street area appears on page 27 and an aerial photo on page 36.

For full details of all other titles still available, special offers, galleries etc., see the website at
paullaceytransportbooks.co.uk

APPENDIX ONE - FLEETS LISTS OF THE LARGER OPERATORS

W. F. CARTER & SONS (ALPHA COACHES), Maidenhead, Berkshire

Reg. No.	Chassis Make & Type	Bodybuilder	Layout	Date New	Date In	Date Out
BL 8538	Crossley WO 25hp ex-WD	??	Ch14	May-21	Mar-23	Sep-32
LW 4396	Crossley X 30hp ex-WD	??	Ch14	Jul-22	Mar-23	??
NO 6432	Crossley WO 25hp ex-WD	Munnion (Chelmsford)	Ch14	Jul-22	c.May -23	??
		re-bodied Furber c/27	ChB14			
??	GMC K16	??	Ch14	??	c.May -23	??
PC 9504	Reo Speed Wagon	??	Ch14	May-23	??/24	??
??	Dennis ex-WD	??	Ch28	??	??	??
PP 7694	Dennis 30cwt	??	C20	Mar-27	Mar-28	??
RX 8407	Commer Invader 6TK	Petty	C20F	Feb-31	New	Jun-45
TY 3085	Leyland Lion PLSC1	LGOC (fiited 1934)	C28R	May-27	??/34	Sep-36
AMO 320	Bedford WTB	Willmott	C26F	May-37	New	Nov-48
RX 6850	Guy OND	Hoyal	B20	May-30	c.Dec/37	Sep-38
JB 5209	Bedford WTL	Duple	C26F	Jul-35	Feb-42	Mar-50
DUU 714	Bedford WTB	Duple	C26F	Apr-37	??/43	Feb-55
CRX 648	Bedford OWB	Duple	B32F	Sep-45	New	??/58
RV 7101	Leyland Cub SKPO3	Duple	C26F	Jul-35	by Feb-46	May-50
UF 8841	Leyland Tiger TS4	Harrington	C32R	Jul-32	Jun-46	Nov-49
DJB 410	Bedford OB	Duple Vista	C29F	Sep-46	New	Mar-60
RX 3633	Thornycroft A2 Long	??	C20	Mar-29	Dec-46	Nov-47
CP 9831	Albion PW65 Valkyrie	Brush	B32F	Jun-32	by Dec-46	Nov-47
EJJ 269	Bedford WTB	Duple	C26F	Sep-37	Oct-47	Feb-53
FLL 58	Bedford WTB MkII	Duple	C26F	Feb-39	Feb-48	Nov-55
HOM 903	Maudslay Marathon MkIII	Burlingham	C33F	Feb-48	Sep-48	May-59
FPU 702	Bedford WTB	Duple	C20F	Nov-37	Nov-48	Feb-55
BDL 111	Bedford WTB	Duple	C26F	Mar-37	Nov-48	Feb-53
MMY 164	Leyland Tiger TS7or8 r/b	Wadham	C33F	Dec-46	Nov-48	Dec-57
EPP 510	Bedford WTB	Duple	C26F	May-38	Nov-48	Mar-53
ERX 432	Dennis Lancet MkII	Willowbrook	C39F	Jul-39	Mar-49	Oct-55
FJB 406	Foden PVSC6	Wadham	C33F	Sep-49	New	Jan-62
FMO 482	Dennis Lancet MkIII	Yeates	C35F	Feb-50	New	Feb-61
FMO 483	Dennis Lancet MkIII	Yeates	C35F	Mar-50	New	Dec-63
FRX 533	Bedford OB	Duple Vista	C29F	Jun-50	New	Oct-64
EUW 51	Bedford WTB	Duple	C25F	Feb-38	Aug-50	Jan-55
DPP 712	Bedford WTB	Willmott	C26R	Jun-37	Feb-51	Nov-52
CYC 421	Dennis Lancet MkII	Dennis	C32C	May-37	Feb-51	Aug-52
GF 5128	AEC Regal 662 (5LW)	Duple (re-bodied 1938)	C32F	Apr-30	May-52	Feb-55
EBU 790	Leyland Tiger PS1/1	Bellhouse Hartwell	C33F	Jul-48	Mar-53	Dec-57
OMP 141	Bedford OB	Duple Vista	C29F	Mar-47	Dec-53	Nov-58
OMP 143	Bedford OB	Duple Vista	C29F	Mar-47	Dec-53	Oct-59
DJB 117	Bedford OB	Duple Vista	C27F	Sep-46	Sep-54	Jul-55
FBL 779	Bedford OB	Duple Vista	C27F	Aug-49	Sep-54	Aug-65
MPP 658	Bedford OB	Duple Vista	C27F	Dec-49	Sep-54	Oct-65
GDL 14	Bedford OB	Duple Vista	C29F	Apr-49	Jan-55	Aug-60
KRX 933	Bedford SBG	Duple Vega	C38F	May-55	New	May-69
KYF 896	Bedford OB	Duple Vista	C29F	Jun-50	Mar-55	May-63
EDL 376	Bedford OB	Duple Vista	C29F	Mar-47	Mar-55	Jun-60
LRX 826	Bedford SBG	Duple Vega	C41F	Nov-56	New	May-72
LRX 827	Bedford SBG	Duple Vega	C41F	Mar-57	New	Jul-69
NHO 189	Bedford SBG	Duple Vega	C38F	Jan-55	May-58	Jul-68
NHO 190	Bedford SBG	Duple Vega	C38F	Jan-55	Jan-58	Jun-62
SUO 826	Bedford SBG	Duple Vega	C36F	May-55	Dec-58	Jun-66
SBL 265	Bedford SB3	Plaxton Consort MkIV	C41F	Mar-59	New	Jun-70
FBL 756	Bedford OB	Duple Vista	C29F	Jul-49	May-59	Apr-64
TKO 665	Bedford SBG	Duple Vega	C36F	Oct-54	May-59	May-59
GGV 822	Bedford SBG	Duple Vega	C36F	Dec-54	May-59	Apr-60
SOU 370	Bedford SB3	Duple Vega	C41F	Jan-58	Oct-59	Oct-72
URX 793	Bedford SB1	Burlingham Seagull 60	C41F	May-60	New	May-70

Reg. No.	Chassis Make & Type	Bodybuilder	Layout	Date New	Date In	Date Out
VOT 507	Bedford SB1	Duple Vega	C41F	Jun-59	Jul-60	Sep-66
XOR 904	Bedford SB1	Plaxton Embassy	C41F	Feb-60	Feb-61	Feb-73
NHO 600	Bedford SBG	Duple Vega	C36F	Feb-55	Feb-61	by??/72
GEF 204	Bedford SB1	Plaxton Consort MkIV	C41F	Mar-59	Dec-61	Jun-70
GEF 203	Bedford SB1	Plaxton Consort MkIV	C41F	Mar-59	Apr-62	Dec-68
849 EBL	Bedford VAL14	Plaxton Panorama	C52F	Jun-63	New	Oct-75
188 CUY	Bedford SB1	Plaxton Embassy	C41F	Feb-61	Mar-64	Feb-73
932 DLK	Bedford VAS1	Duple Bella Vista	C29F	May-62	Oct-64	May-70
OCR 337	Bedford SBG	Duple Vega	C36F	Mar-55	Oct-65	Sep-66
ACE 145B	Bedford SB5	Duple Bella Vega	C41F	Apr-64	Jun-66	Oct-74
939 ECE	Bedford SB5	Duple Bella Vega	C41F	Feb-64	Jul-66	Oct-75
JRX 48D	Bedford VAM5	Plaxton Panorama	C45F	Jul-66	New	Feb-85
JRX 49D	Bedford VAM5	Plaxton Panorama	C45F	Jul-66	New	May-75
CJU 578B	Bedford SB5	Plaxton Embassy MkIV	C41F	Oct-64	Jan-68	Dec-74
4020AW	Bedford SB5	Duple Bella Vega	C41F	Jan-63	Jan-68	Jan-75
6593 MU	Bedford SB5	Duple Bella Vega	C41F	Feb-63	Apr-69	Jul-75
23 JTM	Bedford SB5	Duple Bella Vega	C41F	Apr-63	Jul-69	Nov-75
PUW 33F	Bedford VAM70	Duple Viceroy	C45F	Feb-68	Jul-71	Nov-80
JUV 525D	Bedford VAM14	Duple Bella Venture	C45F	May-66	May-72	May-81
JUV 526D	Bedford VAM14	Duple Bella Venture	C45F	May-66	Jun-72	Jul-77
411 COR	Dennis Loline MkIII	Alexander	H68F	Feb-62	Sep-72	Oct-76
NMU 552E	Bedford VAM14	Duple Viceroy	C45F	Jan-67	Feb-73	Apr-80
NMU 559E	Bedford VAM14	Duple Viceroy	C45F	Jan-67	Feb-73	May-80
VLF 37G	Bedford VAM70	Plaxton Panorama Elite	C45F	Apr-69	Sep-74	Mar-81
HTU 95G	Bedford VAM70	Plaxton Panorama Elite	C45F	Mar-69	Dec-74	Mar-81
HTU 93G	Bedford VAM70	Plaxton Panorama Elite	C45F	Mar-69	May-75	Mar-81
YYX 591H	Bristol LHL6L	Plaxton Panorama Elite	C51F	Jun-70	Apr-76	Sep-77
PGW 646L	Bedford YRQ	Plaxton Pan. Elite MkIII	C45F	Jun-73	Feb-77	Feb-88
PGW 647L	Bedford YRQ	Plaxton Pan. Elite MkIII	C45F	Jun-73	Feb-77	Feb-88
HMV643N	Bedford YRT	Plaxton Supreme	C53F	Apr-75	Sep-77	Oct-88
VTP 879L	Ford Transit	Robin Hood	M12	Sep-72	Oct-77	Jan-87
VKM 963J	Bedford VAM70	Plaxton Pan. Elite MKII	C45F	Aug-70	May-78	Jul-86
MUL 700P	Bedford YMT	Duple Dominant	C53F	Jun-76	Dec-78	Nov-88
YDF 295K	Bedford YRQ	Plaxton Pan. Elite MKII	C45F	Aug-71	May-79	Apr-85
SYU 726S	Bedford YMT	Duple Dominant MkII	C53F	Aug-77	Oct-79	Nov-88
RYL 729R	Bedford YMT	Duple Dominant MkII	C53F	Jul-77	Apr-81	Dec-88
RYL 718R	Bedford YMT	Duple Dominant MkII	C49F	May-77	Apr-81	Dec-88
VBH 592S	Ford Transit	Tricentrol	M12	Sep-77	Nov-81	Nov-88
XYK 743T	Bedford YMT	Duple Dominant MkII	C53F	Aug-78	Jun-82	Nov-88
YYL 781T	Bedford YMT	Duple Dominant MkII	C53F	Apr-79	Apr-85	Nov-88
YYL 784T	Bedford YMT	Duple Dominant MkII	C53F	Apr-79	Apr-85	Nov-88
YEC 21W	Volvo B58-61	Plaxton Supreme	C49FT	Aug-80	Feb-86	Nov-88

Notes	W.F. Carter & Sons ran taxis and funeral cars for many years, but full details are not known.
	There were also removals vans, and details of any known vehicles of all those types
	are included in the main text where known, along with any re-bodyings.
	ERX 432 was formerly registered BNR 526, rebuilt after War Service and re-registered.
	MMY 164 was an Arlington Motors rebuild of a pre-war chassis and rebodied as shown.
	YEC 21W was formerly registered as 6 SVK. NHO 190 ran as Dean Coaches

WEST BROS., (BLUE BUS SERVICE), later BRAY TRANSPORT, Bray, Berkshire

Reg. No.	Chassis Make & Type	Bodybuilder	Layout	Date New	Date In	Date Out
??	Renault car		Car 8	??	??/22	??
MO 3096	Chevrolet B	??	B14R	Apr-24	New	by Sep.30
MO 4888	Chevrolet B	??	B14R	Mar-35	New	Mar-31
MO 5307	Morris-Commercial T	??	B14F	May-25	New	Dec-35
RX 329	Guy OW	??	B20F	Jun-27	New	Sep-38
RX 2558	Bean Model 11	Metcalfe	B20F	Jun-28	New	Dec-41
RX 9046	Commer Invader 6TK	Weymann?	C19F	Jul-31	New	Mar-39
NF 9367	Dennis G	??	B20	Jan-28	??	??

Reg. No.	Chassis Make & Type	Bodybuilder	Layout	Date New	Date In	Date Out
MW 1510	Dennis 30cwt	Short	B18F	Mar-28	??/35	??
RD 5481	Commer Invader	Waveney?	C24F	Jun-34	Aug-39	??
DL 7908	Dennis Lancet N/C	Duple	C26D	May-32	May-41	Jun-49
RD 7766	Dodge F/C	REAL	FC25F	Jun-36	Nov-41	by Jun-48
YW 939	Lancia Pentaoita	London Lorries	C20F	May-28	Jan-39	Jun-41
CJB 352	Bedford OWB	Duple	UB28F	Jul-43	New	May-56
CRX 344	Bedford OWB	Duple	UB32F	Dec-44	New	Feb-55
EJB 271	Bedford OB	Mulliner	B30F	Apr-48	New	Nov-58
FBL 515	Bedford OB	Mulliner	B28F	Jun-49	New	Dec-58
BBW 331	Bedford OWB	Duple	C29F	Jan-43	Sep-49	May-54
JNP 990	Bedford OB	Duple Vista	C29F	Oct-50	Mar-58	May-64
DFE 708	Bedford OB	Duple Vista	C29F	Mar-49	Jul-54	Feb-61
GNM 976	Bedford OB	Duple Vista	C29F	Jun-47	Mar-55	Jul-69
FTK 250	Bedford SB	Burlingham Seagull	C35F	May-53	May-56	Jun-60
KCD 736	Bedford OB	Duple Vista	C29F	Feb-50	May-57	Mar-62
NOR 323	Bedford SBO	Duple Vega	C38F	Mar-55	May-58	Dec-64
ASB 373	Bedford SBO	Duple Vega	C36F	Dec-54	Nov-58	Oct-64
ASB 374	Bedford SBO	Duple Vega	C36F	Dec-54	Dec-58	Jun-63
UUF 535	Bedford SB3	Duple Vega	C41F	Feb-58	Mar-61	Jul-69
OCO 169	Bedford SB1	Duple Vega	C41F	Mar-58	Apr-62	May-68
UOT 587	Bedford SB3	Duple Super Vega	C41F	Apr-59	Dec-62	Oct-72
UDH 740	Bedford SBG	Burlingham Seagull	C36F	Apr-55	Feb-64	Mar-66
42 DOB	Bedford SB3	Duple Super Vega	C41F	Jun-61	Oct-64	Oct-72
8530 HK	Bedford SB1	Duple Vega	C41F	Mar-58	Jan-65	Nov-66
UBU 900	Bedford SB3	Duple Super Vega	C41F	Feb-60	Apr-66	Jul-69
825 MPT	Bedford SB5	Duple Bella Vega	C41F	Dec-63	Nov-66	Apr-69
CUJ 306C	Bedford SB5	Duple Bella Vega	C41F	Mar-65	Mar-68	Apr-69

Notes	GNM 976 was formerly registered HMN 600 when operating on the Isle of Man

A. D. HOOPER & SON (THREE LILIES COACHES), Maidenhead, Berkshire

Reg. No.	Chassis Make & Type	Bodybuilder	Layout	Date New	Date In	Date Out
ME 6153	Crossley WO 20/25hp	Hooper	Ch14	Ex-WD	Mar-23	Sep-30
PP 6265	Reo Pullman	Hooper	AW31D	May-26	Apr-30	??
WL 2187	Daimler CM	Hall Lewis	C26D	Mar-27	May-31	Dec-45
FR 7997	Lancia Pentaiota	??	??	Apr-27	Mar-39	Jun-45
WL 8209	??	??	?26?	c.Oct-29	by Jul-39	??
VO 4394	Crossley Eagle	Taylor	C32F	Jul-30	by ??-46	Jun-51
LJ 1529	Daimler CF6	Duple	C32D	Jul-30	by Jun-46	Jul-50
FRX 598	AEC Regal 0662	Vincent	C33F	Jul-50	New	Aug-56
UL 7131	Leyland Lion PLSC3	Beadle	C28D	Jun-29	Mar-51	Sep-53
KR 9919	AEC Regal	Harrington (r/b 1937)	C32F	Mar-31	Oct-53	Oct-55

Notes	See text for the origins and bodying by the Hoopers of ME 6153 and PP 6265

J. H. HARRIS (PIXEY BUS SERVICE), Maidenhead, later Fifield, Berkshire

Reg. No.	Chassis Make & Type	Bodybuilder	Layout	Date New	Date In	Date Out
??	Renault originally as car	Fancourt & Levington	B14F	??	by Jul-22	??
NK 8073	Chevrolet B	??	C11	Jun-24	Jun-27	Not run
RX 1162	Chevrolet LM	??	B14F	Nov-27	New	Apr-33
YH 7344	Chevrolet LM	??	B14F	Jun-27	Nov-28	Oct-30
RM 3889	Chevrolet LM	??	B14F	May-27	??	Apr-33
TM 1258	Chevrolet LM	??	B14F	Jul-27	??	Apr-33
TW 8979	Chevrolet LM	??	B14F	May-27	Dec-28	Apr-33
VF 3004	Chevrolet LO	Waveney	B14F	Sep-27	??-30	Apr-33
EF 3469	Chevrolet LM	Strachan & Brown	B14F	Apr-27	??-30	Apr-33
RT 4952	Chevrolet LP	??	B14F	Oct-28	??-30	Apr-33

Notes	The Renault was a large touring car used for private hire, later rebodied for use as a bus

FULLER & POMROY (BETA BUS SERVICE), Maidenhead, Berkshire

Reg. No.	Chassis Make & Type	Bodybuilder	Layout	Date New	Date In	Date Out
MO 4927	Reo Speedwagon	??	Ch14	Mar-25	New	Jun-32
??	??	??	Ch14	??	by Apr-25	??
VW 1476	Chevrolet LM	??	B14	Sep-27	Jul-30	Dec-30
VW 6831	Chevrolet LP	??	B14	Oct-28	Mar-31	Sep-34
VW 4772	Reo Sprinter	??	B20	May-28	Jun-31	Jan-35
RX 5946	Chevrolet LQ	??	B14	Jan-30	??/33	??
Notes	The second (unknown) charabanc was part of the partnership set up of one vehicle each.					

CHASTELL & GRAY (DEAN BUS SERVICE), Cookham Dean, Berkshire
J.C. CHASTELL (DEAN LUXURY COACHES), Cookham Dean, Berkshire

Reg. No.	Chassis Make & Type	Bodybuilder	Layout	Date New	Date In	Date Out
RX 3773	Chevrolet LP	??	B14F	Feb-29	New	May-33
RX 4500	Chevrolet LQ	REAL	B14F	May-29	New	Jun-34
UR 1444	Chevrolet LP	??	B14F	Oct-28	??/30	??/33
DJB 117	Bedford OB	Duple Vista	C27F	Sep-46	New	Jul-55
FS 8597	Bedford WLB	Burlingham	C20F	May-34	Mar-47	??
GRE 987	Bedford WTB	Duple	C26F	Jul-38	Nov-48	??
FBL 779	Bedford OB	Duple Vista	C27F	Aug-49	New	C
MPP 658	Bedford OB	Duple Vista	C27F	Dec-49	Sep-50	C
KRX 333	Bedford SB	Duple Vega	C38F	May-55	New	See note
AME 707	Bedford WLB	??	?20?	cMay/33	New	Sep-48
Notes	Chastell sold out to W. F. Carter & Sons in September 1954, vehicles acquired marked C					
	KRX 333 was ordered after the take-over but given the Dean Luxury Coaches fleetname					
	NHO 190 also ran as Dean Coaches - see Carters for fuller details					

J. W. SMITH (PRIDE OF THE GREEN), Wooburn Green, Buckinghamshire

Reg. No.	Chassis Make & Type	Bodybuilder	Layout	Date New	Date In	Date Out
BH 1825	Commer	(Lorry and bus)	B14	Feb-21	New	??
LP 8653	Straker-Squire CO	??	B32	Oct-16	Jul-24	Nov-25
NH 686	Straker-Squire	??	B20	??	??	??
PP 6265	Reo Pullman	??	AW26	May-26	New	??/29
PP 8301	Chevrolet LM	??	C14	May-27	New	??
KX 2273	Chevrolet LQ	??	C14	Mar-29	New	??
KX 4772	Chevrolet U	??	C14	Apr-30	New	??
YW 3479	Reo Pullman	??	C20F	May-28	??	by Sep-52
KX 8621	Bedford WLB	Duple	C20F	May-32	New	by Jun-58
AJB 520	Dennis Lancet	Dennis	C32F	Mar-37	New	Aug-40
HBH 331	Bedford OWB	Duple	UB32F	Dec-43	New	Sep-53
SMF 954	Bedford OB	Duple Vista	C29F	Sep-47	by Jan-52	c. Aug-62
KGH 330	Bedford OB	Duple Vista	C29F	Dec-48	??	c. May-61
PKX 51	Bedford SB	Duple Vega	C35F	May-52	New	Apr-69
RWL 294	Bedford SB	Duple Vega	C33F	Jun-51	Aug-56	??
LEL 882	Bedford SB	Gurning Nutting	C33F	May-51	May-60	Nov-64
XNB 785	Bedford SB3	Duple Vega	C41F	Mar-59	Jun-61	Feb-72
792 XTC	Bedford SB5	Duple (Northern) Firefly	C41F	Feb-62	Aug-62	Jul-72
XFV 509	Bedford SB5	Duple (Northern) Firefly	C41F	Apr-62	May-64	Apr-72
NWR 807	Bedford SBG	Burlingham Seagull	C36F	Mar-54	Jun-65	??/70
JNK 684C	Bedford SB5	Duple Bella Vega	C41F	??/65	Sep-67	Feb-72
CCE 930C	Bedford SB5	Duple Bella Vega	C41F	Mar-65	Apr-69	Mar-72
XWX 910	Bedford SB3	Plaxton Consort MkIV	C41F	May-59	Jun-70	Jan-72

Body codes	Before seating capacity			After seating capacity	
	AW	All-weather coach		C	Centre entrance
	B	Single-deck bus		D	Dual entrance
	C	Saloon coach		F	Front entrance
	Ch	Charabanc		R	Rear entrance
	H	Double-decker bus		T	Toilet fitted
	M	Minibus			
	U	Utility construction			